Series 6

Exam Success

By Lewis Morris

Copyright © Network4Learning, Inc. 2018.

www.insiderswords.com/Series 6

ISBN-13: 978-1983272257

Table of Contents

What is "Insider Language"?

Recent research has confirmed what we have known for decades: The strongest students and leaders in industry have a mastered an Insider Language in their subject and field. This Insider language is made up of the technical terms and vocabulary necessary to communicate effectively in classes or the workplace. For those who master it, learning is easier, faster, and much more enjoyable.

Most students who are surveyed report that the greatest challenge to any course of study is learning the vocabulary. When we examine typical college courses, we discover that there is, on average, 250 Insider Terms a student must learn over the course of a semester. Further, most exams rely heavily on this set of words for assessment purposes. The structure of multiple choice exams lends itself perfectly to the testing of this Insider Language. Students who can differentiate between Insider Language terms can handle challenging exam questions with ease and confidence.

From recent research on learning and vocabulary we have learned:

- Your knowledge of any subject is contained in the content-specific words you know. The more of these terms that you know, the easier it is to understand and recall important information; the easier it will be to communicate your ideas to peers, professors, supervisors, and co-workers. The stronger your content-area vocabulary is, the higher your scores will be on your exams and written assignments.

- Students who develop a strong Insider Language perform better on tests, learn faster, retain more information, and express greater satisfaction in learning.

- Familiarizing yourself with subject-area vocabulary before formal study (pre-learning) is the most effective way to learn this language and reap the most benefit.

- The vocabulary on standardized exams come directly from the stated objectives of the test-makers. This means that the vocabulary found on standardized exams is predictable. Our books focus on this vocabulary.

- Most multiple-choice exams are glorified vocabulary quizzes. Think about the format of a multiple-choice question. The question stem is a definition of a term and the choices (known as distractors) are 4 or 5 similar words. Your task is to differentiate between the meanings of those terms and choose the correct word.

- It takes a person several exposures to a new word to be able to use it with confidence in conversation or in writing. You need to process these words several different ways to make them part of your long-term memory.

The goals of this book are:
- To give you an "Insider Language" for your subject.
- Pre-teach the most important words before you set out on a traditional course of review or study.
- Teach you the most important words in your subject area.
- Teach you strategies for learning subject-area words on your own.
- Boost your confidence in your ability to master this language and support you in your study.
- Reduce the stress of studying and provide you with fun activities that work.

How it works:
The secret to mastering Insider Language is through repetition and exposure. We have eleven steps for you to follow:

1. Read the word and definition in the glossary out loud. "See it, Say it"
2. Identify the part of speech the word belongs to such as noun, verb, adverb, or adjective. This will help you group the word and identify similar words.
3. Place the word in context by using it in a sentence. Write this sentence down and read it aloud.
4. Use "Chunking" to group the words. Make a diagram or word cloud using these groups.
5. Make connections to the words by creating analogies.
6. Create mnemonics that help you recognize patterns and orders of words by substituting the words for more memorable items or actions.
7. Examine the morphology of the word, that is, identify the root, prefix, and suffix that make up the word. Identify similar and related words.
8. Complete word games and puzzles such as crosswords and word searches.
9. Complete matching questions that require you to differentiate between related words.
10. Complete Multiple-choice questions containing the words.
11. Create a visual metaphor or "memory cartoon" to make a mental picture of the word and related processes.

By completing this word study process, you will be exposed to the terminology in various ways that will activate your memory and create a lasting understanding of this language.

The strategies in this book are designed to make you an independent expert at learning insider language. These strategies include:

- Verbalizing the word by reading it and its definition aloud ("See It, Say It"). This allows you to make visual, auditory, and speech connections with its meaning.

- Identifying the type of word (Noun, verb, adverb, and adjective). Making this distinction helps you understand how to visualize the word. It helps you "chunk" the words into groups, and gives you clues on how to use the word.

- Place the word in context by using it in a sentence. Write this sentence down and read it aloud. This will give you an example of how the word is used.

- "Chunking". By breaking down the word list into groups of closely related words, you will learn them better and be able to remember them faster. Once you have group the terms, you can then make word clouds using a free online service. These word clouds provide visual cues to remembering the words and their meanings.

- Analogies. By creating analogies for essential words, you will be making connections that you can see on paper. These connections can trigger your memory and activate your ability to use the word in your writing as you begin to use them. Many of these analogies also use visual cues. In a sense, you can make a mental picture from the analogy.

- Mnemonics. A device such as a pattern of letters, ideas, or associations that assists in remembering something. A mnemonic is especially useful for remembering the order of a set of words or the order of a process.

- Morphology. The study of word roots, prefixes, and suffixes. By examining the structure of the words, you will gain insight into other words that are closely related, and learn how to best use the word.

- Visual metaphors. This is the most sophisticated and entertaining strategy for learning vocabulary. Create a "memory cartoon" using one or more of the vocabulary terms. This activity triggers the visual part of your memory and makes fast, permanent, imprints of the word on your memory. By combining the terms in your visual metaphor, you can "chunk" the entire set of vocabulary terms into several visual metaphors and benefit from the brain's tendency to group these terms.

The activities in this book are designed to imprint the words and their meanings in your memory in different ways. By completing each activity, you will gain the necessary exposures to the word to make it a permanent part of your vocabulary. Each activity uses a different part of your memory. The result is that you will be comfortable using these words and be able to tell the difference between closely related words. The activities include:

A. Crossword Puzzles and Word Searches- These are proven to increase test scores and improve comprehension. Students frequently report that they are fun and engaging, while requiring them to analyze the structure and meaning of the words.

B. Matching- This activity is effective because it forces you to differentiate between many closely related terms.

C. Multiple Choice- This classic question format lends itself to vocabulary study perfectly. Most exams are in this format because they are simple to make, easy to score, and are a reliable type of assessment. (Perfect for the Vocabulary Master!) One strategy to use with multiple choice questions that enhance their effectiveness is to cover the answer choices while you read the question. After reading the question, see if you can answer it before looking at the choices. Then look at the choices to see if you match one of them.

Conducting a thorough "word study" of your insider language will take time and effort, but the rewards will be well worth it. By following this guide and completing the exercises thoughtfully, you will become a stronger, more effective, and satisfied student. Best of luck on your mastery of this Insider Language!

Insider Language Strategies

"See It, Say It!" Reading your Insider Language set aloud

"IT IS BETTER TO FAIL IN ORIGINALITY THAN TO SUCCEED IN IMITATION."
–HERMAN MELVILLE

Reading aloud is the foundation for the development of an Insider Language. It is the single most important thing you can do for vocabulary acquisition. Done correctly, it engages the visual, auditory, and speech centers of the brain and hastens its storage in your long-term memory.

Reading aloud demonstrates the relationship between the printed word and its meaning.

You can read aloud on a higher level than you can initially understand, so reading aloud makes complex ideas more accessible and exposes you to vocabulary and patterns that are not part of your typical speech. Reading aloud helps you understand the complicated text better and makes more challenging text easier to grasp and understand. Reading aloud helps you to develop the "habits of mind" the strongest students use.

Reading aloud will make connections to concepts in the reading that requires you to relate the new vocabulary to things you already know. Go to the glossary at the end of this book and for each word complete the five steps outlined below:

1. Read the word and its definition aloud. Focus on the sound of the word and how it looks on the paper.
2. Read the word aloud again try to say three or four similar words; this will help you build connections to closely related words.
3. Read the word aloud a third time. Try to make a connection to something you have read or heard.
4. Visualize the concept described in the term. Paint a mental picture of the word in use.
5. Try to think of the opposite of the word. Discovering a close antonym will help you place this word in context.

Create a sentence using the word in its proper context

"OPPORTUNITIES DON'T HAPPEN. YOU CREATE THEM." –CHRIS GROSSER

Context means the circumstances that form the setting for an event, statement, or idea, and which it can be fully understood and assessed. Synonyms for context include conditions, factors, situation, background, and setting.
Place the word in context by using it in a sentence. Write this sentence down and read it aloud. By creating sentences, you are practicing using the word correctly. If you strive to make these sentences interesting and creative, they will become more memorable and effective in activating your long-term memory.

Identify the Parts of Speech
"SUCCESS IS NOT FINAL; FAILURE IS NOT FATAL: IT IS THE COURAGE TO CONTINUE THAT COUNTS." –WINSTON S. CHURCHILL

Read through each term in the glossary and make a note of what part of speech each term is. Studying and identifying parts of speech shows us how the words relate to each other. It also helps you create a visualization of each term. Below are brief descriptions of the parts of speech for you to use as a guide.

VERB: A word denoting action, occurrence, or existence. Examples: walk, hop, whisper, sweat, dribbles, feels, sleeps, drink, smile, are, is, was, has.

NOUN: A word that names a person, place, thing, idea, animal, quality, or action. Nouns are the subject of the sentence. Examples: dog, Tom, Florida, CD, pasta, hate, tiger.

ADJECTIVE: A word that modifies, qualifies, or describes nouns and pronouns. Generally, adjectives appear immediately before the words they modify. Examples: smart girl, gifted teacher, old car, red door.

ADVERB: A word that modifies verbs, adjectives and other adverbs. An "ly" ending almost always changes an adjective to an adverb. Examples: ran swiftly, worked slowly, and drifted aimlessly. Many adverbs do not end in "ly." However, all adverbs identify when, where, how, how far, how much, etc. Examples: run hot, lived hard, moved right, study smart.

Chunking

"YOUR POSITIVE ACTION COMBINED WITH POSITIVE THINKING RESULTS IN SUCCESS." SHIV KHERA

Chunking is when you take a set of words and break it down into groups based on a common relationship. Research has shown that our brains learn by chunking information. By grouping your terms, you will be able to recall large sets of these words easily. To help make your chunking go easily use an online word cloud generator to make a set of word clouds representing your chunks.

1. Study the glossary and decide how you want to chunk the set of words. You can group by part of speech, topic, letter of the alphabet, word length, etc. Try to find an easy way to group each term.
2. Once you have your different groups, visit www.wordclouds.com to create a custom word cloud for each group. Print each one of these clouds and post it in a prominent place to serve as constant visual aids for your learning.

Analogies

"CHOOSE THE POSITIVE. YOU HAVE CHOICE, YOU ARE MASTER OF YOUR ATTITUDE, CHOOSE THE POSITIVE, THE CONSTRUCTIVE. OPTIMISM IS A FAITH THAT LEADS TO SUCCESS."– BRUCE LEE

An analogy is a comparison in which an idea or a thing is compared to another thing that is quite different from it. Analogies aim at explaining an idea by comparing it to something that is familiar. Metaphors and similes are tools used to create analogies.

Analogies are useful for learning vocabulary because they require you to analyze a word (or words), and then transfer that analysis to another word. This transfer reinforces the understanding of all the words.

As you analyze the relationships between the analogies you are creating, you will begin to understand the complex relationships between the seemingly unrelated words.

_A_ is to _B_ as _C_ is to _D_

This can be written using colons in place of the terms "is to" and "as."

A:B::C:D

The two items on the left (items A & B) describe a relationship and are separated by a single colon. The two items on the right (items C & D) are shown on the right and are also separated by a colon. Together, both sides are then separated by two colons in the middle, as shown here: Tall: Short :: Skinny: Fat. The relationship used in this analogy is the antonym.

How to create an analogy

Start with the basic formula for an analogy:

____ : ____ :: ____ : ____

Next, we will examine a simple synonym analogy:

automobile : car :: box : crate

The key to figuring out a set of word analogies is determining the relationship between the paired set of words.

Here is a list of the most common types of Analogies and examples

Synonym   Scream : Yell :: Push : Shove

Antonym   Rich : Poor :: Empty : Full

Cause is to Effect   Prosperity : Happiness :: Success : Joy

A Part is to its Whole   Toe : Foot :: Piece : Set

An Object to its Function   Car : Travel :: Read : Learn

A Item is to its Category   Tabby : House Cat :: Doberman : Dog

Word is a symptom of the other   Pain : Fracture :: Wheezing : Allergy

An object and it's description   Glass : Brittle :: Lead : Dense

The word is lacking the second word   Amputee : Limb :: Deaf : Hearing

The first word Hinders the second word   Shackles : Movement :: Stagger : Walk

The first word helps the action of the second Knife : Bread :: Screwdriver : Screw

This word is made up of the second word   Sweater : Wool :: Jeans : Denim

A word and it's definition   Cede: Break Away :: Abolish : To get rid of

Using words from the glossary, make a set of analogies using each one. As a bonus, use more than one glossary term in a single analogy.

_____ : _____ :: _____ : _____

Name the relationship between the words in your analogy:_____

_____ : _____ :: _____ : _____

Name the relationship between the words in your analogy:_____

_____ : _____ :: _____ : _____

Name the relationship between the words in your analogy:_____

Mnemonics

"IT ISN'T THE MOUNTAINS AHEAD TO CLIMB THAT WEAR YOU OUT; IT'S THE PEBBLE IN YOUR SHOE." —MUHAMMAD ALI

A mnemonic is a learning technique that helps you retain and remember information. Mnemonics are one of the best learning methods for remembering lists or processes in order. Mnemonics make the material more meaningful by adding associations and creating patterns. Interestingly, mnemonics may work better when they utilize absurd, startling, or shocking examples and references. Mnemonics help organize the information so that you can easily retrieve it later. By giving you associations and cues, mnemonics allow you to form a mental structure ordering a list or process to help you remember it better. This mental structure allows you to create a structure of association between items that may not appear to have any relationship. Mnemonics typically use references that are easy to visualize and thus easier to remember. Through visualization of vivid images and references, the information is much easier to imprint into long-term memory. The power of making mnemonics lies in converting dull, inert and uninspiring information into something vibrant and memorable.

How to make simple and effective mnemonics
Some of the best mnemonics help us remember simple rules or lists in order.

Step 1. Take a list of terms you are trying to remember in order. For example, we will use the scientific method:

observation, question, hypothesis, methods, results, and conclusion.

Next, we will replace each word on the list with a new word that starts with the same letter. These new words will together form a vivid sentence that is easy to remember:

Objectionable Queens Haunted Macho Rednecks Creatively.

As silly as the above sentence seems, it is easy to remember, and now we can call on this sentence to remind us of the order of the scientific method.

Visit http://www.mnemonicgenerator.com/ and try typing in a list of words. It is fun to see the mnemonics that it makes and shows how easy it is to make great mnemonics to help your studying.

Using vivid words in your mnemonics allows you to see the sentence you are making. Words that are gross, scary, or name interesting animals are helpful. Profanity is also useful because the shock value can trigger memory. The following are lists of vivid words to use in your mnemonics:

Gross words

Moist, Gurgle, Phlegm, Fetus, Curd, Smear, Squirt, Chunky, Orifice, Maggots, Viscous, Queasy, Bulbous, Pustule, Putrid, Fester, Secrete, Munch, Vomit, Ooze, Dripping, Roaches, Mucus, Stink, Stank, Stunk, Slurp, Pus, Lick, Salty, Tongue, Fart, Flatulence, Hemorrhoid.

Interesting Animals

Aardvark, Baboon, Chicken, Chinchilla, Duck, Dragonfly, Emu, Electric Eel, Frog, Flamingo, Gecko, Hedgehog, Hyena, Iguana, Jackal, Jaguar, Leopard, Lynx, Minnow, Manatee, Mongoose, Neanderthal, Newt, Octopus, Oyster, Pelican, Penguin, Platypus, Quail, Racoon, Rattlesnake, Rhinoceros, Scorpion, Seahorse, Toucan, Turkey, Vulture, Weasel, Woodpecker, Yak, Zebra.

Superhero Words

Diabolical, Activate, Boom, Clutch, Dastardly, Dynamic, Dynamite, Shazam, Kaboom, Zip, Zap, Zoom, Zany, Crushing, Smashing, Exploding, Ripping, Tearing.

Scary Words

Apparition, Bat, Chill, Demon, Eerie, Fangs, Genie, Hell, Lantern, Macabre, Nightmare, Owl, Ogre, Phantasm, Repulsive, Scarecrow, Tarantula, Undead, Vampire, Wraith, Zombie.

There are several types of mnemonics that can help your memory.

1. Images

Visual mnemonics are a type of **mnemonic** that works by associating an image with characters or objects whose name sounds like the item that must be memorized. This is one of the easiest ways to create effective mnemonics. An example would be to use the shape of numbers to help memorize a long list of them. Numbers can be memorized by their shapes, so that: 0 -looks like an egg; 1 -a pencil, or a candle; 2 -a snake; 3 -an ear; 4 -a sailboat; 5 -a key; 6 -a comet; 7 -a knee; 8 -a snowman; 9 -a comma.

Another type of visual mnemonic is the word-length mnemonic in which the number of letters in each word corresponds to a digit. This simple mnemonic gives pi to seven decimal places:

3.141582 becomes "How I wish I could calculate pi."

Of course, you could use this type of mnemonic to create a longer sentence showing the digits of an important number. Some people have used this type of mnemonic to memorize thousands of digits.

Using the hands is also an important tool for creating visual objects. Making the hands into specific shapes can help us remember the pattern of things or the order of a list of things.

2. Rhyming

Rhyming mnemonics are quick ways to make things memorable. A classic example is a mnemonic for the number of days in each month:
"30 days hath September, April, June, and November.
All the rest have 31
Except February, my dear son.
It has 28, and that is fine
But in Leap Year it has 29."

Another example of a rhyming mnemonic is a common spelling rule:
"I before e except after c
or when sounding like a
in neighbor and weigh."

Use **rhymer.com** to get large lists of rhyming words.

3. Homonym

A homonym is one of a group of words that share the same pronunciation but have different meanings, whether spelled the same or not.

Try saying what you're attempting to remember out loud or very quickly, and see if anything leaps out. If you know other languages, using similar-sounding words from those can be effective.

You could also browse this list of homonyms at http://www.cooper.com/alan/homonym_list.html.

4. Onomatopoeia

An Onomatopeia is a word that phonetically imitates, resembles or suggests the source of the sound that it describes. Are there any noises made by the thing you're trying to memorize? Is it often associated with some other sound? Failing that, just make up a noise that seems to fit.

Achoo, ahem, baa, bam, bark, beep, beep beep, belch, bleat, boo, boo hoo, boom, burp, buzz, chirp, click clack, crash, croak, crunch, cuckoo, dash, drip, ding dong, eek, fizz, flit, flutter, gasp, grrr, ha ha, hee hee, hiccup, hiss, hissing, honk, icky, itchy, jiggly, jangle, knock knock, lush, la la la, mash, meow, moan, murmur, neigh, oink, ouch, plop, pow, quack, quick, rapping, rattle, ribbit, roar, rumble, rustle, scratch, sizzle, skittering, snap crackle pop, splash, splish splash, spurt, swish, swoosh, tap, tapping, tick tock, tinkle, tweet, ugh, vroom, wham, whinny, whip, whooping, woof.

5. Acronyms

An acronym is a word or name formed as an abbreviation from the initial components of a word, such as NATO, which stands for North Atlantic Treaty Organization. If you're trying to memorize something involving letters, this is often a good bet. A lot of famous mnemonics are acronyms, such as ROYGBIV which stands for the order of colors in the light spectrum (Red, Orange, Yellow, Green, Blue, Indigo, and Violet).
A great acronym generator to try is: www.all-acronyms.com.

A different spin on an acronym is a backronym. A **backronym** is a specially constructed phrase that is supposed to be the source of a word that is an acronym. A backronym is constructed by creating a new phrase to fit an already existing word, name, or acronym.

The word is a combination of *backward* and *acronym*, and has been defined as a "reverse acronym." For example, the United States Department of Justice assigns to their Amber Alert program the meaning "**A**merica's **M**issing: **B**roadcast **E**mergency **R**esponse." The process can go either way to make good mnemonics.

Visit: https://arthurdick.com/projects/backronym/ to try out a simple backronym generator.

6. Anagrams

An anagram is a direct word switch or word play, the result of rearranging the letters of a word or phrase to produce a new word or phrase, using all the original letters exactly once; for example, the word anagram can be rearranged into nag-a-ram.

Try re-arranging letters or components and see if anything memorable emerges. Visit http://www.nameacronym.net/ to use a simple anagram generator.

One particularly memorable form of anagram is the spoonerism, where you swap the initial syllables or letters of words to make new phrases. These are usually humorous, and this makes them easier to remember. Here are some examples:

"Is it kisstomary to cuss the bride?" (as opposed to "customary to kiss")
"The Lord is a shoving leopard." (instead of "a loving shepherd")
"A blushing crow." ("crushing blow")
"A well-boiled icicle" ("well-oiled bicycle")
"You were fighting a liar in the quadrangle." ("lighting a fire")
"Is the bean dizzy?" (as opposed to "is the dean busy?")

7. Stories

Make up quick stories or incidents involving the material you want to memorize. For larger chunks of information, the stories can get more elaborate. Structured stories are particularly good for remembering lists or other sequenced information. Have a look at https://en.wikipedia.org/wiki/Method_of_loci for a more advanced memory sequencing technique.

Visual Metaphors

"LIMITS, LIKE FEAR, IS OFTEN AN ILLUSION." –MICHAEL JORDAN

What is a Metaphor?

A metaphor is a figure of speech that refers to one thing by mentioning another thing. Metaphors provide clarity and identify hidden similarities between two seemingly unrelated ideas. A visual metaphor is an image that creates a link between different ideas.

Visual metaphors help us use our understanding of the world to learn new concepts, skills, and ideas. Visual metaphors help us relate new material to what we already know. Visual metaphors must be clear and simple enough to spark a connection and understanding. Visual metaphors should use familiar things to help you be less fearful of new, complex, or challenging topics. Metaphors trigger a sense of familiarity so that you are more accepting of the new idea. Metaphors work best when you associate a familiar, easy to understand idea with a challenging, obscure, or abstract concept.

How to make a visual metaphor

1. Brainstorm using the words of the concept. Use different fonts, colors, or shapes to represent parts of the concept.

2. Merge these images together

3. Show the process using arrows, accents, etc.

4. Think about the story line your metaphor projects.

Examples of visual metaphors:

A skeleton used to show a framework of something.

A cloud showing an outline.

A bodybuilder whose muscles represent supporting ideas and details.

A sandwich where the meat, tomato, and lettuce represent supporting ideas.

A recipe card to show a process.

Your metaphor should be accurate. It should be complex enough to convey meaning, but simple and clear enough to be easily understood.

Morphology
"SCIENCE IS THE CAPTAIN, AND PRACTICE THE SOLDIERS." LEONARDO DA VINCI

Morphology is the study of the origin, roots, suffixes, and prefixes of the words. Understanding the meaning of prefixes, suffixes, and roots make it easier to decode the meaning of new vocabulary. Having the ability to decode using morphology increases text comprehension when initially reading as well.

The capability of identifying meaningful parts of words (morphemes), including prefixes, suffixes, and roots can be helpful. Identifying morphemes improves decoding accuracy and fluency. Reading speed improves when you can decode larger chunks of text quickly. When you can recognize morphemes in words, you will be better able to make sense of new words in context. Below are charts containing the most common prefixes, suffixes, and root words. Use them to help you decode your vocabulary terms.

Prefixes

Prefix	Meaning	Example words and meanings	
a, ab, abs	away from	absent abdicate	not to be present, to give up an office or throne.
ad, a, ac, af, ag, an, ar, at, as	to, toward	Advance advantage	To move forward To have the upper hand
anti	against	Antidote antisocial antibiotic	To repair poisoning refers to someone who's not social
bi, bis	two	bicycle binary biweekly	two-wheeled cycle two number system every two weeks
circum, cir	around	circumnavigate circle	Travel around the world a figure that goes all around
com, con, co, col	with, together	Complete Complement	To finish To go along with
de	away from, down, the opposite of	depart detour	to go away from to go out of your way
dis, dif, di	apart	dislike dishonest distant	not to like not honest away
En-, em-	Cause to	Entrance	the way in.
epi	upon, on top of	epitaph epilogue epidemic	writing upon a tombstone speech at the end, on top of the rest
equ, equi	equal	equalize equitable	to make equal fair, equal
ex, e, ef	out, from	exit eject exhale	to go out to throw out to breathe out
Fore-	Before	Forewarned	To have prior warning

Prefix	Meaning	Example Words and Meanings	
in, il, ir, im, en	in, into	Infield Imbibe	The inner playing field to take part in
in, il, ig, ir, im	not	inactive ignorant irreversible irritate	not active not knowing not reversible to put into discomfort
inter	between, among	international interact	among nations to mix with
mal, male	bad, ill, wrong	malpractice malfunction	bad practice fail to function, bad function
Mid	Middle	Amidships	In the middle of a ship
mis	wrong, badly	misnomer	The wrong name
mono	one, alone, single	monocle	one lensed glasses
non	not, the reverse of	nonprofit	not making a profit
ob	in front, against, in front of, in the way of	Obsolete	No longer needed
omni	everywhere, all	omnipresent omnipotent	always present, everywhere all powerful
Over	On top	Overdose	Take too much medication
Pre	Before	Preview	Happens before a show.
per	through	Permeable pervasive	to pass through, all encompassing
poly	many	Polygamy polygon	many spouses figure with many sides
post	after	postpone postmortem	to do after after death
pre	before, earlier than	Predict Preview	To know before To view before release
pro	forward, going ahead of, supporting	proceed pro-war promote	to go forward supporting the war to raise or move forward
re	again, back	retell recall reverse	to tell again to call back to go back
se	apart	secede seclude	to withdraw, become apart to stay apart from others
Semi	Half	Semipermeable	Half-permeable

Prefix	Meaning	Example Words and Meanings	
Sub	under, less than	Submarine	under water
super	over, above, greater	superstar superimpose	a start greater than her stars to put over something else
trans	across	transcontinental transverse	across the continent to lie or go across
un, uni	one	unidirectional unanimous unilateral	having one direction sharing one view having one side
un	not	uninterested unhelpful unethical	not interested not helpful not ethical

Roots

Root	Meaning	Example words & meanings	
act, ag	to do, to act	Agent Activity	One who acts as a representative Action
Aqua	Water	Aquamarine	The color of water
Aud	To hear	Auditorium	A place to hear music
apert	open	Aperture	An opening
bas	low	Basement Basement	Something that is low, at the bottom A room that is low
Bio	Living thing	Biological	Living matter
cap, capt, cip, cept, ceive	to take, to hold, to seize	Captive Receive Capable Recipient	One who is held To take Able to take hold of things One who takes hold or receives
ced, cede, ceed, cess	to go, to give in	Precede Access Proceed	To go before Means of going to To go forward
Cogn	Know	Cognitive	Ability to think
cred, credit	to believe	Credible Incredible Credit	Believable Not believable Belief, trust
curr, curs, cours	to run	Current Precursory Recourse	Now in progress, running Running (going) before To run for aid
Cycle	Circle	Lifecycle	The circle of life
dic, dict	to say	Dictionary Indict	A book explaining words (sayings)

Root	Meaning	Examples and meanings	
duc, duct	to lead	Induce Conduct Aqueduct	To lead to action To lead or guide Pipe that leads water somewhere
equ	equal, even	Equality Equanimity	Equal in social, political rights Evenness of mind, tranquility
fac, fact, fic, fect, fy	to make, to do	Facile Fiction Factory Affect	Easy to do Something that is made up Place that makes things To make a change in
fer, ferr	to carry, bring	Defer Referral	To carry away Bring a source for help/information
Gen	Birth	Generate	To create something
graph	write	Monograph Graphite	A writing on a particular subject A form of carbon used for writing
Loc	Place	Location	A place
Mater	Mother	Maternity	Expecting birth
Mem	Recall	Memory	The recall experiences
mit, mis	to send	Admit Missile	To send in Something sent through the air
Nat	Born	Native	Born in a place
par	equal	Parity Disparate	Equality No equal, not alike
Ped	Foot	Podiatrist	Foot doctor
Photo	Light	Photograph	A picture
plic	to fold, to bend, to turn	Complicate Implicate	To fold (mix) together To fold in, to involve
pon, pos, posit, pose	to place	Component Transpose Compose Deposit	A part placed together with others A place across To put many parts into place To place for safekeeping
scrib, script	to write	Describe Transcript Subscription	To write about or tell about A written copy A written signature or document
sequ, secu	to follow	Sequence	In following order

Root	Meaning	Examples and Meanings	
Sign	Mark	Signal	to alert somebody
spec, spect, spic	to appear, to look, to see	Specimen Aspect	An example to look at One way to see something
sta, stat, sist,	to stand, or make stand	Constant	Standing with
stit, sisto	Stable, steady	Status Stable Desist	Social standing Steady (standing) To stand away from
Struct	To build	Construction	To build a thing
tact	to touch	Contact Tactile	To touch together To be able to be touched
ten, tent, tain	to hold	Tenable Retentive Maintain	Able to be held, holding Holding To keep or hold up
tend, tens, tent	to stretch	Extend Tension	To stretch or draw out Stretched
Therm	Temperature	Thermometer	Detects temperature
tract	to draw	Attract Contract	To draw together An agreement drawn up
ven, vent	to come	Convene Advent	To come together A coming
Vis	See	Invisible	Cannot be seen
ver, vert, vers	to turn	Avert Revert Reverse	To turn away To turn back To turn around

Crossword Puzzles

1. *Using the Across and Down clues, write the correct words in the numbered grid below.*

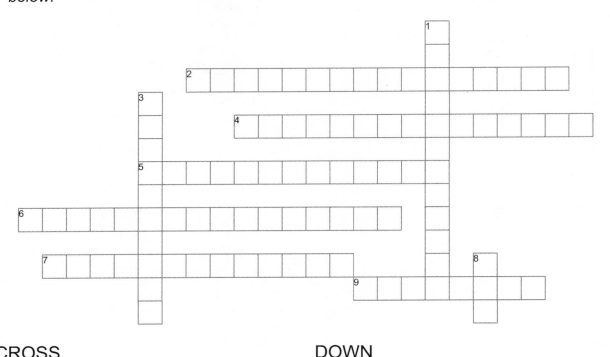

ACROSS

2. Rise in general level of prices reduces the value of fixed returns.
4. Authorized stock is the maximum number of shares a corporation may issue under the terms of its charter.
5. New issue market, primary distribution, sold by prospectus only.
6. Traditionally, the 20-day period between the filing date of a registration statement and the effective date of the registration.
7. Where new issues of stock are issued. The only time when issuing companies make a profit on their shares.
9. A type of mutual fund whose investment policy is to provide stable income with a minimum of capital risks.

DOWN

1. The yield of the security when bought or sold prior to maturity in the secondary market. Current yield relates current income to the security's current price.
3. Nominal Yield
8. Own, Hold, Purchase, Long

A. Current Yield   B. Cooling off Period   C. Authorized Stock   D. Inflationary Risk
E. Primary market   F. Buy   G. Primary Market   H. Coupon Rate
I. Bond Fund

2. *Using the Across and Down clues, write the correct words in the numbered grid below.*

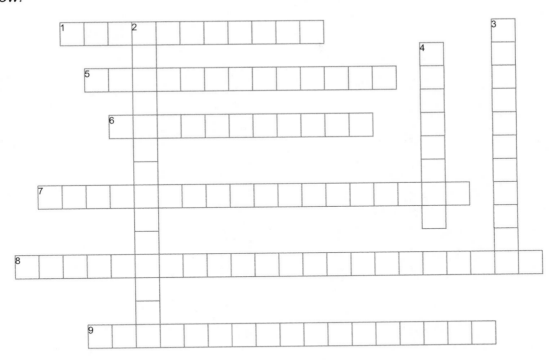

ACROSS

1. State securities laws.
5. A stock exchange where the securities are sold to the highest bidder.
6. Principal Risk
7. Any institution or an individual meeting minimum net worth requirements for the purchase of securities qualifying under the Regulation D registration exemption.
8. Corporate bonds rate BB
9. Shares held by the public

DOWN

2. Auction market
3. A form of business organization in which the total worth of the organization is divided into shares of stock.
4. Measure of the bond price in relations to the time the bond end. Taking in consideration the interest-rates, time to maturity, and differences between the coupon rate and the yield to maturity.

A. Accredited Investor
D. Corporate High Yield Fund
G. Outstanding shares

B. Duration
E. Auction Market
H. Corporation

C. Capital Risk
F. Blue Sky Laws
I. Exchange market

3. *Using the Across and Down clues, write the correct words in the numbered grid below.*

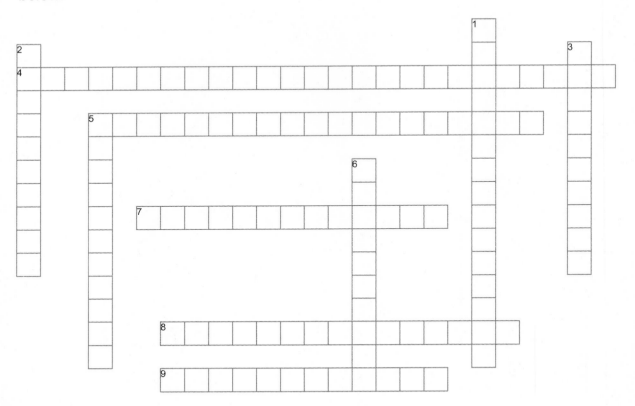

ACROSS

4. Portfolio characterized by high turnover of holdings, attempts to cash in on higher-risk rapid capital appreciation situations.

5. Form of debt backed by stocks and or bonds of another corporation. The collateral is held by a trustee for safekeeping.

7. A theory behind Subchapter M under which distributions to shareholders are not taxed to the investment company.

8. The number of shares of stock that a corporation may issue.

9. Payment of a debt (principal) over a period of time in periodic installments.

DOWN

1. Authorized stock is the maximum number of shares a corporation may issue under the terms of its charter.

2. Possible loss of value due to a broad market decline. For equities, this risk is measured by a statistic called beta.

3. Investing in a specific security at an inopportune time. Dollar cost averaging is used to avoid this risk.

5. Principal Risk

6. Often called "Indirect Debt."

A. Capital Risk
D. Aggressive Growth Portfolio
G. Collateral Trust Bond
J. Timing Risk

B. Market Risk
E. Amortization
H. Authorized Stock

C. Conduit Theory
F. Agency Debt
I. Authorized Stock

4. Using the Across and Down clues, write the correct words in the numbered grid below.

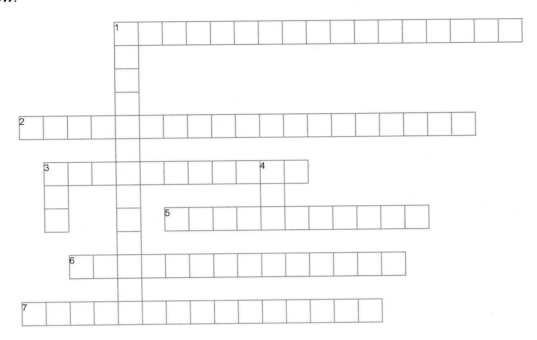

ACROSS

1. A transaction in which a broker or dealer acts for the accounts of others by buying or selling securities on behalf of customers.

2. Loss of income or appreciation because an investment was NOT made.

3. A day the New York Stock Exchange is open for business (trading).

5. General term for possible loss of money invested. This risk is present in most securities.

6. Fixed-Income Securities: Possibility that homeowners will prepay mortgages more quickly than expected when interest rates fall.

7. Investment objective for increase in invested capital, primarily generated through price appreciation. Equity securities (stocks) are usually used in pursuit of this goal.

DOWN

1. Any promotional material designed for use by newspapers, magazines, billboards, radio, television, telephone recordings or other public media.

3. Own, Hold, Purchase, Long

4. Alternative Minimum Tax. The requirement to add the income from tax preference items to income above an indexed level. A method to insure that wealthy persons and corporations pay at least some tax.

A. Buy
D. Business Day
G. Prepayment Risk

B. Growth Objective
E. AMT
H. Agency Transaction

C. Opportunity Cost Risk
F. Advertisement
I. Capital Risk

5. *Using the Across and Down clues, write the correct words in the numbered grid below.*

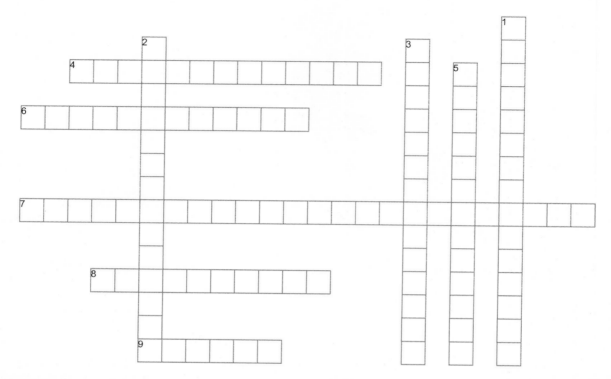

ACROSS

4.   Ability to quickly sell an investment at or near current market price. Regardless of type, more heavily traded securities are more liquid.

6.   Cost basis

7.   Refers to Corporate stocks

8.   Common stock; capital appreciation; income not a consideration; subject to market fluctuations.

9.   Is the price difference the Market Maker is willing to buy the stock for, to the amount he

DOWN

1.   Dollars adjusted to show the same purchasing power from one period to another. They are "indexed" for inflation.

2.   Tax-free bonds

3.   Bank buys issuing companies shares and sells them on the market for commission. Shares are not owned by the banks.

5.   A market in which buyers enter competitive bids and sellers enter competitive offers simultaneously.

A. Constant dollars
D. Contribution
G. Firm Commitment

B. Liquidity Risk
E. Regular way Settlement Date
H. Growth Fund

C. Spread
F. Municipal bonds
I. Auction Market

6. *Using the Across and Down clues, write the correct words in the numbered grid below.*

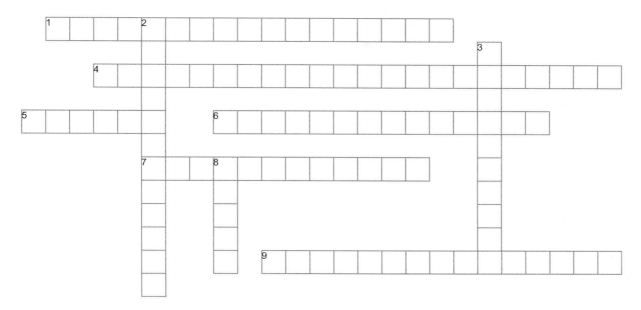

ACROSS

1. Income that is free from federal, and possibly state income tax; higher the investor's tax bracket, the more beneficial the tax exemption; may have some default risk; interest rate risk.

4. The annual meeting that all registered representatives and principals must attend, the purpose of which is to review compliance issues.

5. One who deals in securities as a principal, buying and selling for his own account.

6. The sale of investment company shares in amounts just below the point at which the sales charge is reduced on quantity.

7. Mix of equities and bonds; growth with opportunity for income; portfolio mix usually under tighter constraints than growth & income fund.

9. The interest that has accumulated since the last interest payment up to, but not including, the settlement date, and that is added to a bond transaction's contract price.

DOWN

2. Cost basis

3. The schedule of sales charge discounts offered by a mutual fund for lump sum or cumulative investments. Eligibility requirements must be disclosed in the prospectus.

8. Anything that an individual or a corporation owns.

A. Asset
D. Accrued Interest
G. Contribution

B. Breakpoint
E. Breakpoint Sale
H. Annual Compliance Review

C. Balanced Fund
F. Municipal Bond Fund
I. Dealer

7. *Using the Across and Down clues, write the correct words in the numbered grid below.*

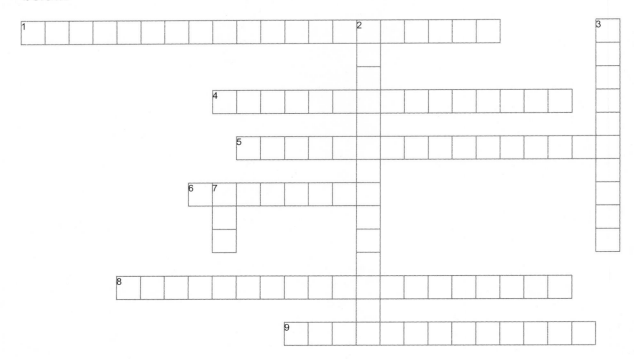

ACROSS

1. Investment objective for investors that are willing and able to take considerable risks for the chance to hit a big financial home run.

4. "New" stock

5. Includes an investment adviser, officer, director, partner or employee of another person.

6. The price at which a dealer is willing to buy stock from an individual or another dealer.

8. A mutual fund that splits its investment assets among stocks, bonds, and other vehicles in an attempt to provide a consistent return for the investor.

9. The stock of normally strong, well-established companies that have demonstrated their ability to pay dividends in good times and bad times.

DOWN

2. The date the security trades without its dividends. In order to get a dividend the security needs to be purchased two days prior to the record date or before the ex-dividend date.

3. A document accompanying or part of a stock certificate that is signed by the person named on the certificate for the purpose of transferring the certificate's title to another person's name.

7. Primary Offering. New issues that are offered in the primary market and are sold to the public for the first time.

A. Asset Allocation Fund
D. Speculation Objective
G. IPO

B. Bid Price
E. Affiliated Person
H. Blue Chip Stock

C. Ex dividend Date
F. Authorized stock
I. Assignment

8. *Using the Across and Down clues, write the correct words in the numbered grid below.*

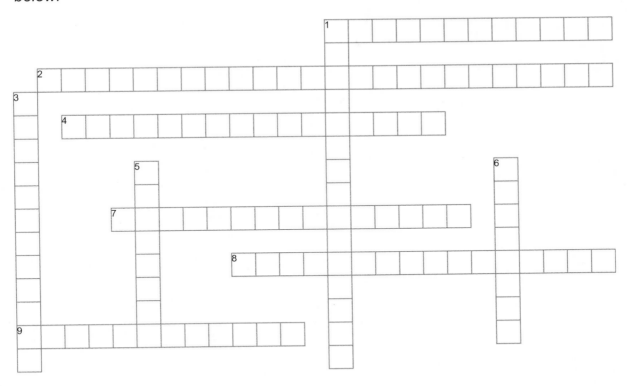

ACROSS

1. Payment of a debt (principal) over a period of time in periodic installments.

2. Refers to Corporate stocks

4. A type of shareholder voting in which the number of shares held is multiplied by the number of directors to be elected to determine the number of votes a shareholder may cast.

7. Investment objective for increase in invested capital, primarily generated through price appreciation. Equity securities (stocks) are usually used in pursuit of this goal.

8. Introduces new securities to the market, that advises the issuing company of the price the security will be sold for to the public.

9. Changes in value of a currency versus another currency. Current owners of forign securities may see a negative impact if foreign currency weakens against their home currency.

DOWN

1. The number of shares of stock that a corporation may issue.

3. A bond's average price is calculated by adding its face value to the price paid for it and dividing the result by two.

5. Measure of the bond price in relations to the time the bond end. Taking in consideration the interest-rates, time to maturity, and differences between the coupon rate and the yield to maturity.

6. Face amount, principal

A. Cumulative Voting
D. Average Price
G. Investment Banker
J. Growth Objective

B. Authorized Stock
E. Amortization
H. Duration

C. Currency Risk
F. Par value
I. Regular way Settlement Date

9. *Using the Across and Down clues, write the correct words in the numbered grid below.*

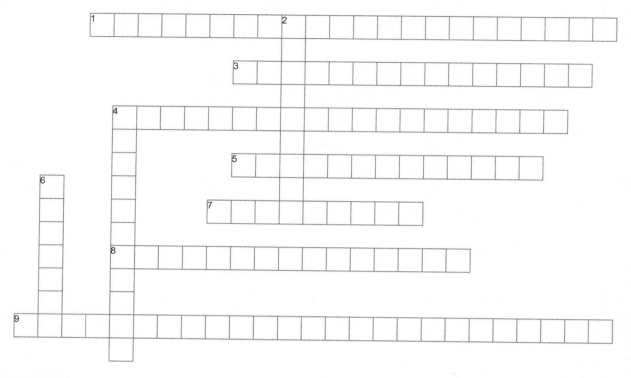

ACROSS

1. Issued by most commercial banks, representing bank borrowing for a short period of time.

3. A bond that may be exchanged for some other security of the issuer at the option of the holder. It is usually converted into common stock based upon a fixed conversion ratio.

4. The net rate of investment return that must be credited to a variable life insurance policy to ensure that at all times the variable death benefit equals the amount of the death benefit.

5. New issue market, primary distribution, sold by prospectus only.

7. Educational IRA

8. Calculation of a bonds total return if held until the end of its life (maturity).

9. A negotiable certificate representing a given number of shares of stock in a foreign corporation.

DOWN

2. To change an annuity contract from the accumulation (pay-in) stage to the distribution (payout) stage.

4. An accounting measure used to determine the amount of each payment during an annuity's distribution stage.

6. Bonds that cost more than the face value.

A. Annuity Unit
D. Assumed Interest Rate
G. Convertible Bond
J. Coverdell

B. Premium
E. Certification of Deposit
H. Yield to maturity

C. Annuitize
F. American Depositary Receipt
I. Primary market

10. *Using the Across and Down clues, write the correct words in the numbered grid below.*

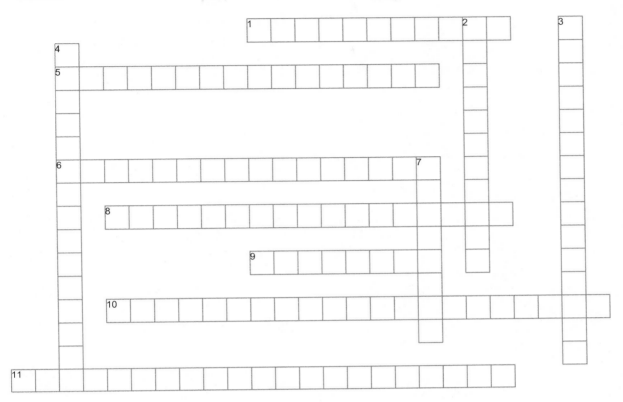

ACROSS

1. A day the New York Stock Exchange is open for business (trading).
5. Traditionally, the 20-day period between the filing date of a registration statement and the effective date of the registration.
6. Growth and income fund
8. Selection risk, business risk
9. Bonds that are sold less then par value.
10. Red Herring
11. An option available to mutual fund shareholders whereby fund dividends and capital gains distributions are automatically reinvested back into the fund.

DOWN

2. An agency Transaction
3. T-bonds, T-notes, T-bills; Income with no credit risk; may be subject to interest rate risk; the longer average maturity of the portfolio the greater the interest rate risk
4. The interest that has accumulated since the last interest payment up to, but not including, the settlement date, and that is added to a bond transaction's contract price.
7. Measure of the bond price in relations to the time the bond end. Taking in consideration the interest-rates, time to maturity, and differences between the coupon rate and the yield to maturity.

A. Agency Basis
D. Non-systematic risk
G. Automatic Reinvestment
J. Business Day

B. Discount
E. Preliminary prospectus
H. US Goverment Fund
K. Equity income fund

C. Cooling off Period
F. Accrued Interest
I. Duration

11. *Using the Across and Down clues, write the correct words in the numbered grid below.*

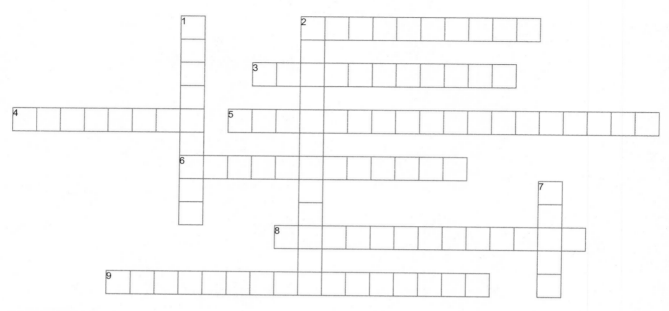

ACROSS

2. Often called "Indirect Debt."
3. Principal Risk
4. Face amount, principal
5. Provides a method of handling securities-related disputes or clearing controversies between members, public customers, clearing corporations or clearing banks.
6. Payment of a debt (principal) over a period of time in periodic installments.
8. Ability to quickly sell an investment at or near current market price. Regardless of type, more heavily traded securities are more liquid.
9. Introduces new securities to the market, that advises the issuing company of the price the security will be sold for to the public.

DOWN

1. Date transaction is executed.
2. The increase in value of an asset. Sometimes called growth.
7. Anything that an individual or a corporation owns.

A. Trade date
E. Agency Debt
I. Asset
B. Par value
F. Amortization
J. Code of Arbitrations
C. Liquidity Risk
G. Appreciation
D. Capital Risk
H. Investment Banker

12. *Using the Across and Down clues, write the correct words in the numbered grid below.*

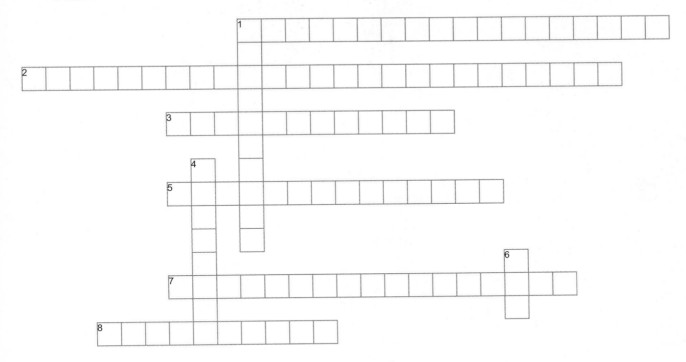

ACROSS

1. Provides a method of handling securities-related disputes or clearing controversies between members, public customers, clearing corporations or clearing banks.

2. Portfolio characterized by high turnover of holdings, attempts to cash in on higher-risk rapid capital appreciation situations.

3. Coupon, coupon rate, interest

5. The date the security trades without its dividends. In order to get a dividend the security needs to be purchased two days prior to the record date or before the ex-dividend date.

7. Common stocks from outside of the U.S.; Exposure to exchange rate risk and political (legistlative) risk, in addition to market risk.

8. Systematic risk

DOWN

1. Possibility that principal or interest will not be paid.

4. Switch

6. Own, Hold, Purchase, Long

A. Nominal yield
D. Aggressive Growth Portfolio
G. Market risk

B. International Fund
E. Buy
H. Code of Arbitrations

C. Exchange
F. Credit Risk
I. Ex dividend Date

13. *Using the Across and Down clues, write the correct words in the numbered grid below.*

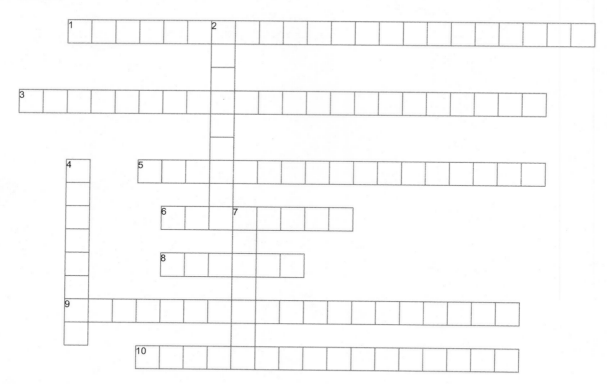

ACROSS

1. Issued by most commercial banks, representing bank borrowing for a short period of time.
3. Corporate bonds rate BB
5. The period during which contributions are made to an annuity account.
6. The price at which a dealer is willing to buy stock from an individual or another dealer.
8. Is the price difference the Market Maker is willing to buy the stock for, to the amount he
9. Has the right to receive skipped or missed dividends.
10. An accounting measure used to determine an annuitant's proportionate interest in the insurer's separate account during an annuity's accumulation (deposit) stage.

DOWN

2. Equity Category; Portfolio: common stock in same proportions as selected index.
4. The price at which the dealer is willing to sell the stock to an investor or another dealer.
7. Bonds that cost more than the face value.

A. Ask Price
D. Certification of Deposit
G. Bid Price
J. Accumulation Unit

B. Accumulation Stage
E. Corporate High Yield Fund
H. Index Fund

C. Spread
F. Cumulative Preferred
I. Premium

14. *Using the Across and Down clues, write the correct words in the numbered grid below.*

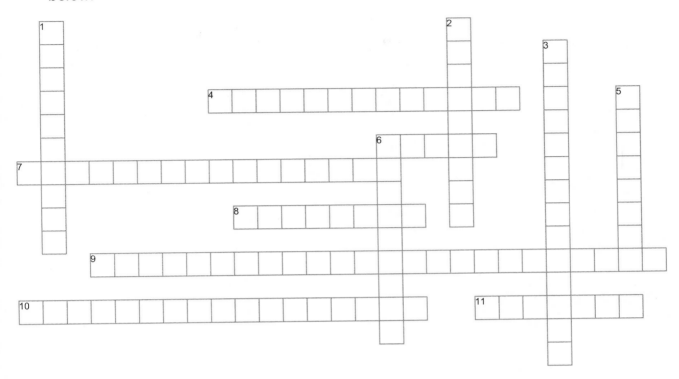

ACROSS

4. The stock of normally strong, well-established companies that have demonstrated their ability to pay dividends in good times and bad times.

6. An individual or a firm that effects securities transactions for the accounts of others.

7. Includes an investment adviser, officer, director, partner or employee of another person.

8. Face amount, principal

9. Refers to Corporate stocks

10. Mix of equities and bonds.

11. Bank End Load

DOWN

1. Open end management company.

2. States that the issuing company wants ALL (or nothing) the shares to be sold if not, the underwriting is cancelled.

3. Date transaction is completed and the seller pays buyer and the buyer receives the shares.

5. Bonds that are sold less then par value.

6. Person who receives an annuity contract's distribution.

A. Mutual Fund
D. Blue Chip Stock
G. Settlement date
J. Affiliated Person

B. Agent
E. Regular way Settlement Date
H. All or none
K. Annuitant

C. Growth & Income Fund
F. Par value
I. Discount
L. B shares

15. *Using the Across and Down clues, write the correct words in the numbered grid below.*

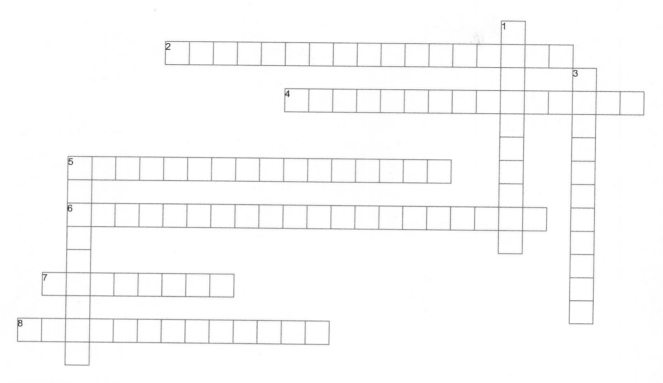

ACROSS

2. Essentially a letter of credit from a bank guaranteeing payment of a debt.
4. The date the Board of Directors announces intention of paying dividends.
5. Articles of Incorporation
6. Possible large gain if situation plays out as manager predicts; Depends on ability of manager to find special deals.
7. Bonds are more likely to be called when rates have dropped, forcing reinvestment of principal at lower rates.
8. New issue market, primary distribution, sold by prospectus only.

DOWN

1. Adjustment bond
3. Principal Risk
5. Money on which taxes have been paid. A return of cost basis is a return of capital and not subject to tax.

A. Declaration Date
D. Corporate Charter
G. Bankers Acceptance

B. Primary market
E. Capital Risk
H. Call Risk

C. Special Situation Fund
F. Income bond
I. Cost Basis

16. *Using the Across and Down clues, write the correct words in the numbered grid below.*

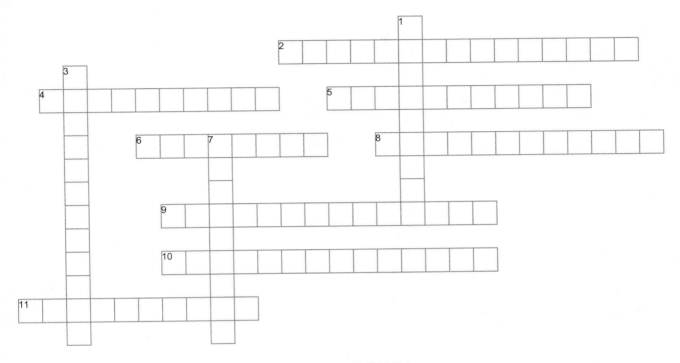

ACROSS

2. Authorized stock is the maximum number of shares a corporation may issue under the terms of its charter.

4. A creditor

5. A day the New York Stock Exchange is open for business (trading).

6. Measure of the bond price in relations to the time the bond end. Taking in consideration the interest-rates, time to maturity, and differences between the coupon rate and the yield to maturity.

8. Sales Charge, Sales Load

9. Graduated tax, income tax

10. Tax-free bonds

11. Common stock; capital appreciation; income not a consideration; subject to market fluctuations.

DOWN

1. The technique of buying and selling the same financial instrument in two different markets simultaneously to take advantage of a momentary price disparity.

3. Cost basis

7. States that the issuing company wants ALL (or nothing) the shares to be sold if not, the underwriting is cancelled.

A. Progressive tax
E. Municipal bonds
I. Growth Fund

B. Business Day
F. All or none
J. Brokerage fee

C. Duration
G. Arbitrage
K. Authorized Stock

D. Contribution
H. Bondholder

17. *Using the Across and Down clues, write the correct words in the numbered grid below.*

ACROSS

3. Rise in general level of prices reduces the value of fixed returns.

5. Yield stated on the bonds coupon.

6. Principal

9. Articles of Incorporation

10. Income that is free from federal, and possibly state income tax; higher the investor's tax bracket, the more beneficial the tax exemption; may have some default risk; interest rate risk.

DOWN

1. General term for possible loss of money invested. This risk is present in most securities.

2. An accounting measure used to determine an annuitant's proportionate interest in the insurer's separate account during an annuity's accumulation (deposit) stage.

4. Common stock from particular industry.

7. Bonds that cost more than the face value.

8. Possible loss of value due to a broad market decline. For equities, this risk is measured by a statistic called beta.

11. Own, Hold, Purchase, Long

A. Inflationary Risk
D. Market Risk
G. Corporate Charter
J. Capital Risk

B. Dealer
E. Municipal Bond Fund
H. Premium
K. Buy

C. Nominal yield
F. Sector Fund
I. Accumulation Unit

18. *Using the Across and Down clues, write the correct words in the numbered grid below.*

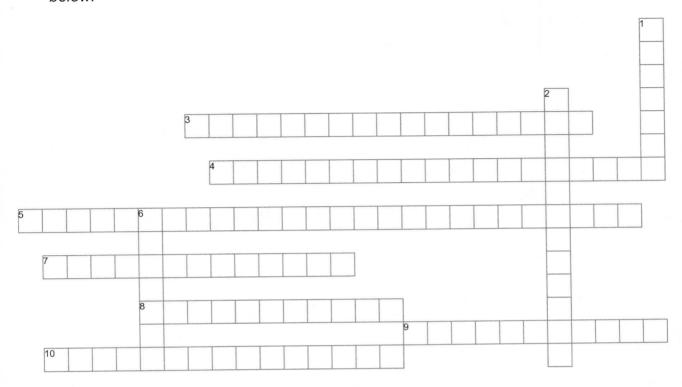

ACROSS

3. Common stocks from outside of the U.S.; Exposure to exchange rate risk and political (legistlative) risk, in addition to market risk.

4. A debt security backed by a loan, lease or receivables against assets other than real estate and mortgage-backed securities.

5. A policy concentrating on maximum return. Such a policy entails increased risks.

7. Where new issues of stock are issued. The only time when issuing companies make a profit on their shares.

8. Wholesaler, sponsor, underwriter

9. Buys stocks for its clients and for personal needs based on their listing price on the floor.

10. Cash equivalents such as T-bills, CDs, commercial paper, BAs; Preservation of Capital; attempts to maintain $1 NAV ; used to park funds while making investment decisions.

DOWN

1. A contract between an insurance company and an individual, generally guaranteeing lifetime income to the individual.

2. Holding period return

6. Allows the Underwriting firm to purchase any shares that the issuing company's shareholders have not bought and sell the shares themselves for a profit.

A. International Fund
D. Asset Backed Security
G. Floor Broker
J. Annual return

B. Primary Market
E. Aggressive Investment Policy
H. Standby

C. Distributor
F. Annuity
I. Money Market Fund

19. *Using the Across and Down clues, write the correct words in the numbered grid below.*

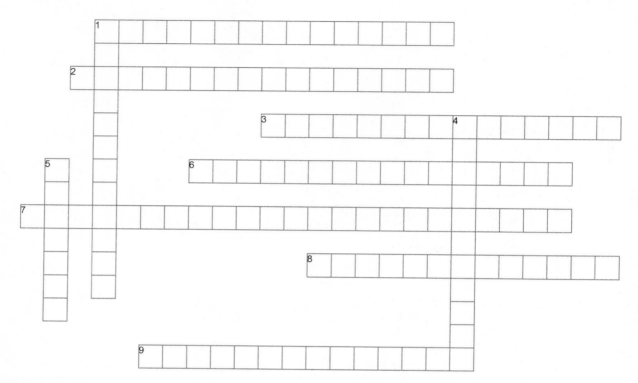

ACROSS

1. The number of shares of stock that a corporation may issue.

2. Traditionally, the 20-day period between the filing date of a registration statement and the effective date of the registration.

3. Calculation of a bonds total return if held until the end of its life (maturity).

6. An accounting measure used to determine an annuitant's proportionate interest in the insurer's separate account during an annuity's accumulation (deposit) stage.

7. Acting as an agent for the issuer, the underwriter puts forth his or her best efforts to sell as many shares as possible.

8. New issue market, primary distribution, sold by prospectus only.

9. Auction market

DOWN

1. Payment of a debt (principal) over a period of time in periodic installments.

4. An accounting measure used to determine the amount of each payment during an annuity's distribution stage.

5. A price at a midpoint among a number of prices. Technical analysts often use averages as market indicators.

A. Best Efforts Underwriting
D. Primary market
G. Accumulation Unit
J. Exchange market

B. Yield to maturity
E. Annuity Unit
H. Authorized Stock

C. Amortization
F. Cooling off Period
I. Average

20. *Using the Across and Down clues, write the correct words in the numbered grid below.*

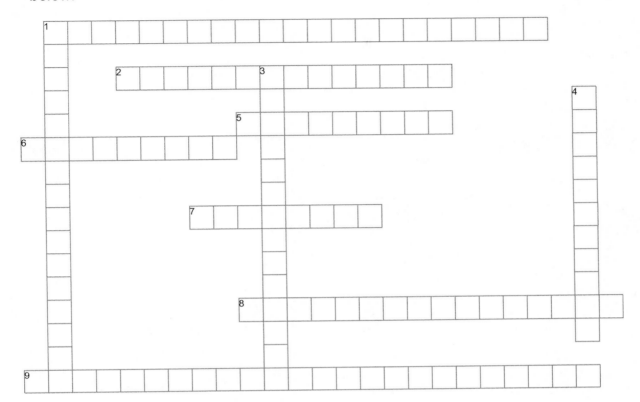

ACROSS

1. An option available to mutual fund shareholders whereby fund dividends and capital gains distributions are automatically reinvested back into the fund.

2. Fixed-Income Securities: Possibility that homeowners will prepay mortgages more quickly than expected when interest rates fall.

5. To change an annuity contract from the accumulation (pay-in) stage to the distribution (payout) stage.

6. Person who receives an annuity contract's distribution.

7. The price at which a dealer is willing to buy stock from an individual or another dealer.

8. Articles of Incorporation

9. Refers to Corporate stocks

DOWN

1. Registered Representative

3. Tax-free bonds

4. Broker-dealer firm primarily on the NASDAQ that opens bids and sells a particular security, taking on the risk of selling that security.

A. Annuitize
D. Municipal bonds
G. Regular way Settlement Date
J. Bid Price

B. Annuitant
E. Automatic Reinvestment
H. Corporate Charter

C. Prepayment Risk
F. Market Maker
I. Account Executive

21. *Using the Across and Down clues, write the correct words in the numbered grid below.*

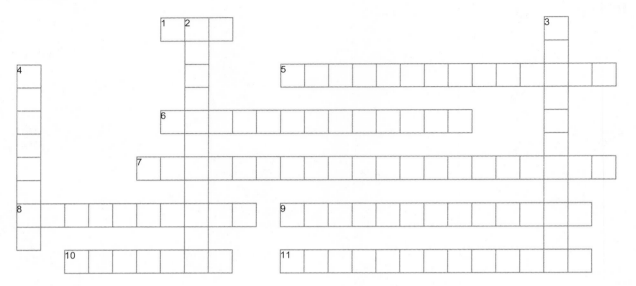

ACROSS

1. Primary Offering. New issues that are offered in the primary market and are sold to the public for the first time.

5. Bank buys issuing companies shares and sells them on the market for commission. Shares are not owned by the banks.

6. The price of a mutual fund. Calculates to company's funds minus liabilities divided by outstanding shares.

7. Investment objective for a combination of growth of capital and income, but less of each than investments that focus on just one of those objectives.

8. Nominal Yield

9. Changes in laws or rules may have negative impact on investments. The common wisdom is that political risk is high anytime Congress is in session.

10. Bank End Load

11. Where new issues of stock are issued. The only time when issuing companies make a profit on their shares.

DOWN

2. The date the company mails out the dividend.

3. A debt security issued by an authorized agency of the federal government.

4. The price at which a dealer is willing to buy stock from an individual or another dealer.

A. Total Return Objective
D. Bid Price
G. Payment date
J. Coupon Rate

B. Net Asset Value
E. B shares
H. Agency Issue
K. IPO

C. Primary Market
F. Political Risk
I. Firm Commitment

22. *Using the Across and Down clues, write the correct words in the numbered grid below.*

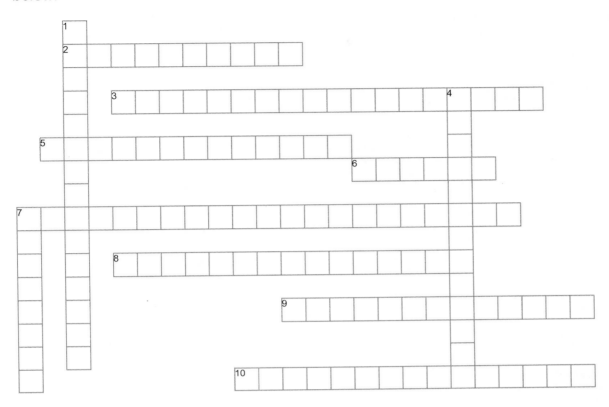

ACROSS

2. Common stock from particular industry.
3. Contingent deferred sales charge (CDSC)
5. The price of a mutual fund. Calculates to company's funds minus liabilities divided by outstanding shares.
6. An agent
7. Red Herring
8. Dollars adjusted to show the same purchasing power from one period to another. They are "indexed" for inflation.
9. A market in which buyers enter competitive bids and sellers enter competitive offers simultaneously.
10. Calculation of a bonds total return if held until the end of its life (maturity).

DOWN

1. T-bonds, T-notes, T-bills; Income with no credit risk; may be subject to interest rate risk; the longer average maturity of the portfolio the greater the interest rate risk
4. Any material designed for use by newspapers, magazines, radio, television, telephone, recordings or any other public medium to solicit business.
7. Face amount, principal

A. Preliminary prospectus
D. Sector Fund
G. Net Asset Value
J. Par value

B. US Goverment Fund
E. Advertisement
H. Constant dollars
K. Auction Market

C. Back end sales charge
F. Broker
I. Yield to maturity

23. *Using the Across and Down clues, write the correct words in the numbered grid below.*

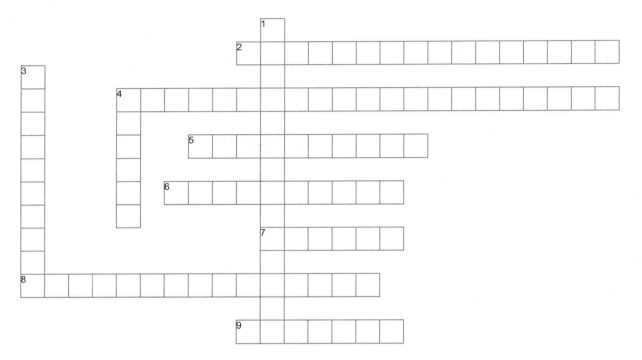

ACROSS

2. A type of shareholder voting in which the number of shares held is multiplied by the number of directors to be elected to determine the number of votes a shareholder may cast.

4. Red Herring

5. A document accompanying or part of a stock certificate that is signed by the person named on the certificate for the purpose of transferring the certificate's title to another person's name.

6. Open end management company.

7. The role of a brokerage firm when it acts as an agent for a customer and charges the customer a commission for its services.

8. The date on which the company declares an upcoming dividend.

9. Bank End Load

DOWN

1. Tax-free bonds

3. Common stock from inside and outside the U.S. Capital appreciation in whatever markets look attractive to manager.

4. Tax- deductible

A. Mutual Fund
D. Broker
G. B shares
J. Preliminary prospectus

B. Declaration Date
E. Global Fund
H. Assignment

C. Cumulative Voting
F. Pre-tax
I. Municipal bonds

24. *Using the Across and Down clues, write the correct words in the numbered grid below.*

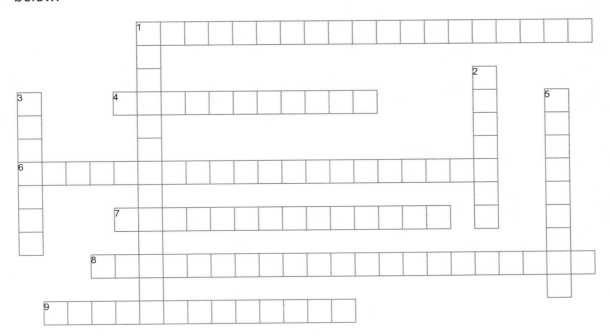

ACROSS

1. The net rate of investment return that must be credited to a variable life insurance policy to ensure that at all times the variable death benefit equals the amount of the death benefit.

4. Wholesaler, sponsor, underwriter

6. Small cap stocks; maximum capital appreciation; may employ short-term trading strategies; very volatile.

7. Fixed-Income Securities: Possibility that homeowners will prepay mortgages more quickly than expected when interest rates fall.

8. An option available to mutual fund shareholders whereby fund dividends and capital gains distributions are automatically reinvested back into the fund.

9. Any material designed for use by newspapers, magazines, radio, television, telephone, recordings or any other public medium to solicit business.

DOWN

1. A person authorized by a court of law to liquidate an intestate decedent's estate.

2. Allows the Underwriting firm to purchase any shares that the issuing company's shareholders have not bought and sell the shares themselves for a profit.

3. Level Load

5. A type of best efforts underwriting where the entire amount must be sold or the deal is called off.

A. C shares
D. Standby
G. Prepayment Risk
J. All or None

B. Aggressive Growth Fund
E. Advertisement
H. Assumed Interest Rate

C. Automatic Reinvestment
F. Administrator
I. Distributor

25. *Using the Across and Down clues, write the correct words in the numbered grid below.*

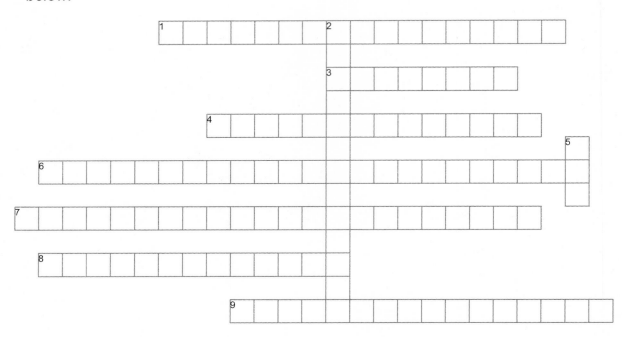

ACROSS

1. The period during which contributions are made to an annuity account.

3. Excessive trading in a customer's account. The registered representative ignores the objectives and interest of clients and seeks only to increase commissions.

4. Tax-free bonds

6. Acting as an agent for the issuer, the underwriter puts forth his or her best efforts to sell as many shares as possible.

7. A unit investment trust with which an investor may contact to buy mutual fund shares at fixed intervals over a fixed period of time.

8. Changes in laws or rules may have negative impact on investments. The common wisdom is that political risk is high anytime Congress is in session.

9. Dividend paying equities; safe, consistent income with secondary objective of growth; less volatile than other equity funds.

DOWN

2. A stock exchange where the securities are sold to the highest bidder.

5. Adjusted Gross Income. Earned income plus net passive income, portfolio income, and capital gains.

A. Municipal bonds
D. Contractual Plan Company
G. AGI

B. Churning
E. Best Efforts Underwriting
H. Accumulation Stage

C. Political Risk
F. Equity Income Fund
I. Auction Market

1. *Using the Across and Down clues, write the correct words in the numbered grid below.*

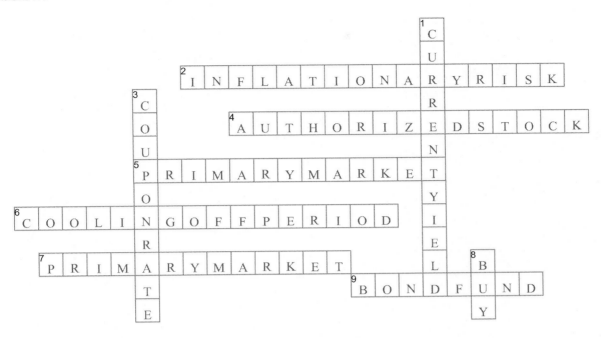

ACROSS

2. Rise in general level of prices reduces the value of fixed returns.

4. Authorized stock is the maximum number of shares a corporation may issue under the terms of its charter.

5. New issue market, primary distribution, sold by prospectus only.

6. Traditionally, the 20-day period between the filing date of a registration statement and the effective date of the registration.

7. Where new issues of stock are issued. The only time when issuing companies make a profit on their shares.

9. A type of mutual fund whose investment policy is to provide stable income with a minimum of capital risks.

DOWN

1. The yield of the security when bought or sold prior to maturity in the secondary market. Current yield relates current income to the security's current price.

3. Nominal Yield

8. Own, Hold, Purchase, Long

A. Current Yield
E. Primary market
I. Bond Fund

B. Cooling off Period
F. Buy

C. Authorized Stock
G. Primary Market

D. Inflationary Risk
H. Coupon Rate

2. *Using the Across and Down clues, write the correct words in the numbered grid below.*

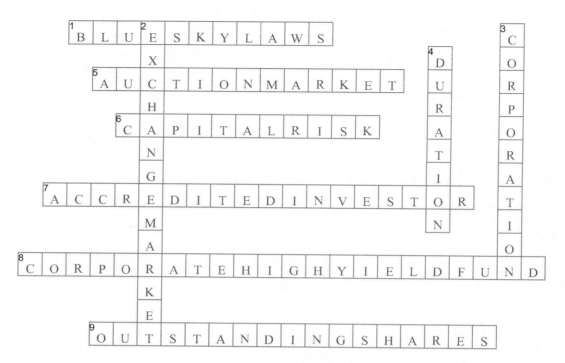

ACROSS

1. State securities laws.
5. A stock exchange where the securities are sold to the highest bidder.
6. Principal Risk
7. Any institution or an individual meeting minimum net worth requirements for the purchase of securities qualifying under the Regulation D registration exemption.
8. Corporate bonds rate BB
9. Shares held by the public

DOWN

2. Auction market
3. A form of business organization in which the total worth of the organization is divided into shares of stock.
4. Measure of the bond price in relations to the time the bond end. Taking in consideration the interest-rates, time to maturity, and differences between the coupon rate and the yield to maturity.

A. Accredited Investor
D. Corporate High Yield Fund
G. Outstanding shares

B. Duration
E. Auction Market
H. Corporation

C. Capital Risk
F. Blue Sky Laws
I. Exchange market

3. Using the Across and Down clues, write the correct words in the numbered grid below.

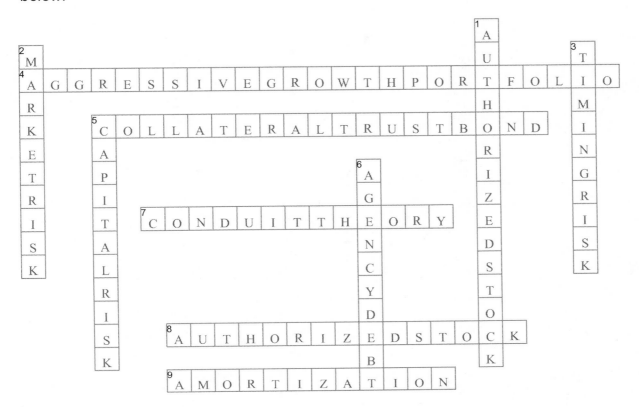

ACROSS

4. Portfolio characterized by high turnover of holdings, attempts to cash in on higher-risk rapid capital appreciation situations.

5. Form of debt backed by stocks and or bonds of another corporation. The collateral is held by a trustee for safekeeping.

7. A theory behind Subchapter M under which distributions to shareholders are not taxed to the investment company.

8. The number of shares of stock that a corporation may issue.

9. Payment of a debt (principal) over a period of time in periodic installments.

DOWN

1. Authorized stock is the maximum number of shares a corporation may issue under the terms of its charter.

2. Possible loss of value due to a broad market decline. For equities, this risk is measured by a statistic called beta.

3. Investing in a specific security at an inopportune time. Dollar cost averaging is used to avoid this risk.

5. Principal Risk

6. Often called "Indirect Debt."

A. Capital Risk
D. Aggressive Growth Portfolio
G. Collateral Trust Bond
J. Timing Risk

B. Market Risk
E. Amortization
H. Authorized Stock

C. Conduit Theory
F. Agency Debt
I. Authorized Stock

4. *Using the Across and Down clues, write the correct words in the numbered grid below.*

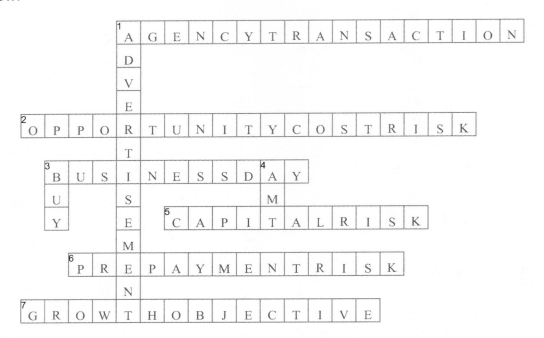

ACROSS

1. A transaction in which a broker or dealer acts for the accounts of others by buying or selling securities on behalf of customers.

2. Loss of income or appreciation because an investment was NOT made.

3. A day the New York Stock Exchange is open for business (trading).

5. General term for possible loss of money invested. This risk is present in most securities.

6. Fixed-Income Securities: Possibility that homeowners will prepay mortgages more quickly than expected when interest rates fall.

7. Investment objective for increase in invested capital, primarily generated through price appreciation. Equity securities (stocks) are usually used in pursuit of this goal.

DOWN

1. Any promotional material designed for use by newspapers, magazines, billboards, radio, television, telephone recordings or other public media.

3. Own, Hold, Purchase, Long

4. Alternative Minimum Tax. The requirement to add the income from tax preference items to income above an indexed level. A method to insure that wealthy persons and corporations pay at least some tax.

A. Buy
D. Business Day
G. Prepayment Risk

B. Growth Objective
E. AMT
H. Agency Transaction

C. Opportunity Cost Risk
F. Advertisement
I. Capital Risk

5. *Using the Across and Down clues, write the correct words in the numbered grid below.*

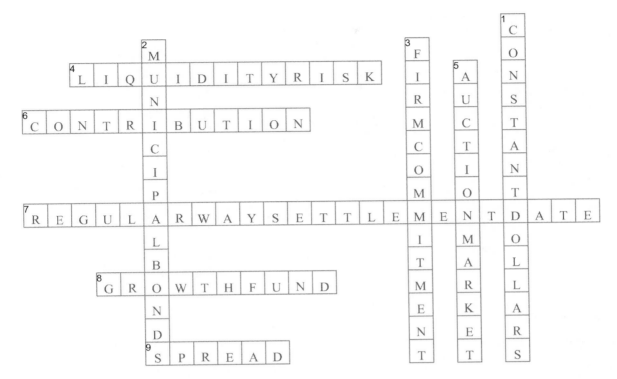

ACROSS

4. Ability to quickly sell an investment at or near current market price. Regardless of type, more heavily traded securities are more liquid.

6. Cost basis

7. Refers to Corporate stocks

8. Common stock; capital appreciation; income not a consideration; subject to market fluctuations.

9. Is the price difference the Market Maker is willing to buy the stock for, to the amount he

DOWN

1. Dollars adjusted to show the same purchasing power from one period to another. They are "indexed" for inflation.

2. Tax-free bonds

3. Bank buys issuing companies shares and sells them on the market for commission. Shares are not owned by the banks.

5. A market in which buyers enter competitive bids and sellers enter competitive offers simultaneously.

A. Constant dollars
D. Contribution
G. Firm Commitment
B. Liquidity Risk
E. Regular way Settlement Date
H. Growth Fund
C. Spread
F. Municipal bonds
I. Auction Market

6. *Using the Across and Down clues, write the correct words in the numbered grid below.*

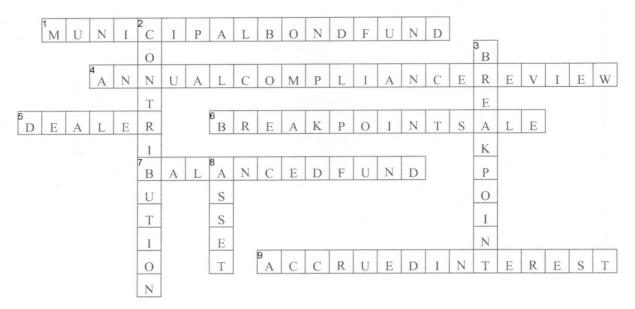

ACROSS

1. Income that is free from federal, and possibly state income tax; higher the investor's tax bracket, the more beneficial the tax exemption; may have some default risk; interest rate risk.

4. The annual meeting that all registered representatives and principals must attend, the purpose of which is to review compliance issues.

5. One who deals in securities as a principal, buying and selling for his own account.

6. The sale of investment company shares in amounts just below the point at which the sales charge is reduced on quantity.

7. Mix of equities and bonds; growth with opportunity for income; portfolio mix usually under tighter constraints than growth & income fund.

9. The interest that has accumulated since the last interest payment up to, but not including, the settlement date, and that is added to a bond transaction's contract price.

DOWN

2. Cost basis

3. The schedule of sales charge discounts offered by a mutual fund for lump sum or cumulative investments. Eligibility requirements must be disclosed in the prospectus.

8. Anything that an individual or a corporation owns.

A. Asset
D. Accrued Interest
G. Contribution

B. Breakpoint
E. Breakpoint Sale
H. Annual Compliance Review

C. Balanced Fund
F. Municipal Bond Fund
I. Dealer

7. *Using the Across and Down clues, write the correct words in the numbered grid below.*

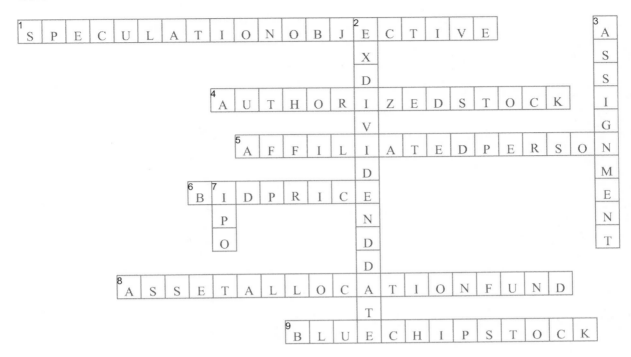

ACROSS

1. Investment objective for investors that are willing and able to take considerable risks for the chance to hit a big financial home run.

4. "New" stock

5. Includes an investment adviser, officer, director, partner or employee of another person.

6. The price at which a dealer is willing to buy stock from an individual or another dealer.

8. A mutual fund that splits its investment assets among stocks, bonds, and other vehicles in an attempt to provide a consistent return for the investor.

9. The stock of normally strong, well-established companies that have demonstrated their ability to pay dividends in good times and bad times.

DOWN

2. The date the security trades without its dividends. In order to get a dividend the security needs to be purchased two days prior to the record date or before the ex-dividend date.

3. A document accompanying or part of a stock certificate that is signed by the person named on the certificate for the purpose of transferring the certificate's title to another person's name.

7. Primary Offering. New issues that are offered in the primary market and are sold to the public for the first time.

A. Asset Allocation Fund
D. Speculation Objective
G. IPO

B. Bid Price
E. Affiliated Person
H. Blue Chip Stock

C. Ex dividend Date
F. Authorized stock
I. Assignment

8. *Using the Across and Down clues, write the correct words in the numbered grid below.*

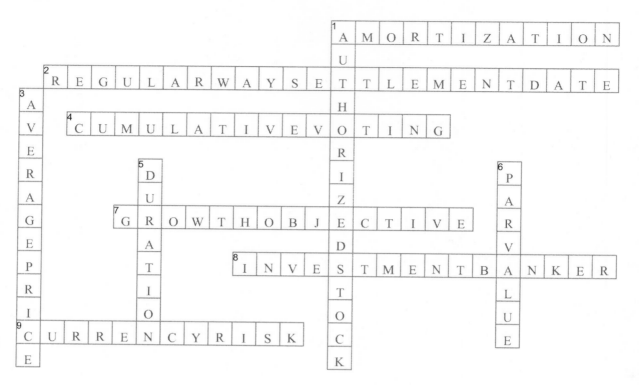

ACROSS

1. Payment of a debt (principal) over a period of time in periodic installments.

2. Refers to Corporate stocks

4. A type of shareholder voting in which the number of shares held is multiplied by the number of directors to be elected to determine the number of votes a shareholder may cast.

7. Investment objective for increase in invested capital, primarily generated through price appreciation. Equity securities (stocks) are usually used in pursuit of this goal.

8. Introduces new securities to the market, that advises the issuing company of the price the security will be sold for to the public.

9. Changes in value of a currency versus another currency. Current owners of forign securities may see a negative impact if foreign currency weakens against their home currency.

DOWN

1. The number of shares of stock that a corporation may issue.

3. A bond's average price is calculated by adding its face value to the price paid for it and dividing the result by two.

5. Measure of the bond price in relations to the time the bond end. Taking in consideration the interest-rates, time to maturity, and differences between the coupon rate and the yield to maturity.

6. Face amount, principal

A. Cumulative Voting
D. Average Price
G. Investment Banker
J. Growth Objective

B. Authorized Stock
E. Amortization
H. Duration

C. Currency Risk
F. Par value
I. Regular way Settlement Date

9. *Using the Across and Down clues, write the correct words in the numbered grid below.*

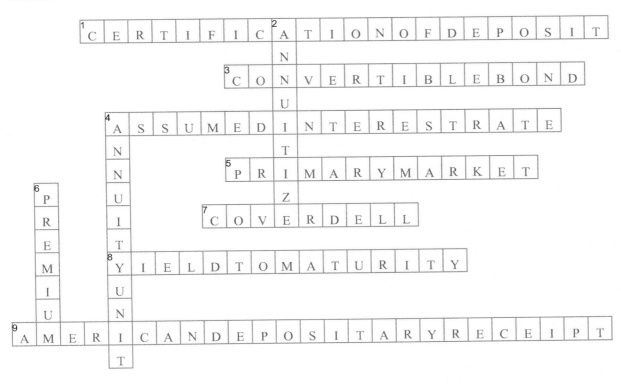

ACROSS

1. Issued by most commercial banks, representing bank borrowing for a short period of time.

3. A bond that may be exchanged for some other security of the issuer at the option of the holder. It is usually converted into common stock based upon a fixed conversion ratio.

4. The net rate of investment return that must be credited to a variable life insurance policy to ensure that at all times the variable death benefit equals the amount of the death benefit.

5. New issue market, primary distribution, sold by prospectus only.

7. Educational IRA

8. Calculation of a bonds total return if held until the end of its life (maturity).

9. A negotiable certificate representing a given number of shares of stock in a foreign corporation.

DOWN

2. To change an annuity contract from the accumulation (pay-in) stage to the distribution (payout) stage.

4. An accounting measure used to determine the amount of each payment during an annuity's distribution stage.

6. Bonds that cost more than the face value.

A. Annuity Unit
D. Assumed Interest Rate
G. Convertible Bond
J. Coverdell

B. Premium
E. Certification of Deposit
H. Yield to maturity

C. Annuitize
F. American Depositary Receipt
I. Primary market

10. *Using the Across and Down clues, write the correct words in the numbered grid below.*

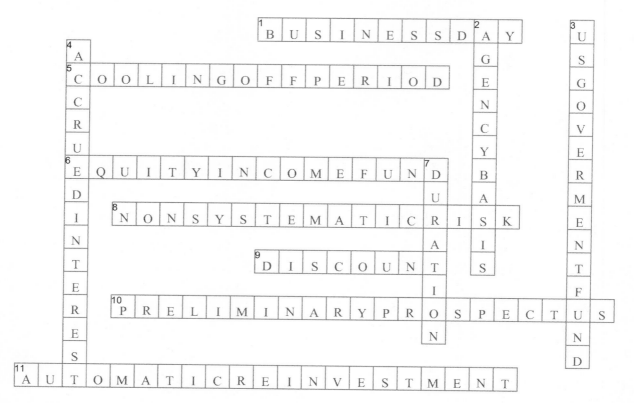

ACROSS

1. A day the New York Stock Exchange is open for business (trading).
5. Traditionally, the 20-day period between the filing date of a registration statement and the effective date of the registration.
6. Growth and income fund
8. Selection risk, business risk
9. Bonds that are sold less then par value.
10. Red Herring
11. An option available to mutual fund shareholders whereby fund dividends and capital gains distributions are automatically reinvested back into the fund.

DOWN

2. An agency Transaction
3. T-bonds, T-notes, T-bills; Income with no credit risk; may be subject to interest rate risk; the longer average maturity of the portfolio the greater the interest rate risk
4. The interest that has accumulated since the last interest payment up to, but not including, the settlement date, and that is added to a bond transaction's contract price.
7. Measure of the bond price in relations to the time the bond end. Taking in consideration the interest-rates, time to maturity, and differences between the coupon rate and the yield to maturity.

A. Agency Basis
D. Non-systematic risk
G. Automatic Reinvestment
J. Business Day

B. Discount
E. Preliminary prospectus
H. US Goverment Fund
K. Equity income fund

C. Cooling off Period
F. Accrued Interest
I. Duration

11. *Using the Across and Down clues, write the correct words in the numbered grid below.*

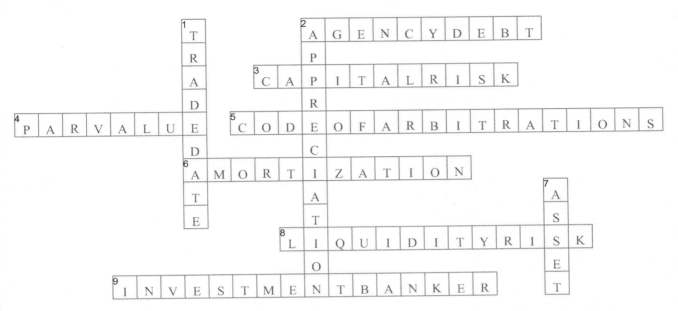

ACROSS

2. Often called "Indirect Debt."

3. Principal Risk

4. Face amount, principal

5. Provides a method of handling securities-related disputes or clearing controversies between members, public customers, clearing corporations or clearing banks.

6. Payment of a debt (principal) over a period of time in periodic installments.

8. Ability to quickly sell an investment at or near current market price. Regardless of type, more heavily traded securities are more liquid.

9. Introduces new securities to the market, that advises the issuing company of the price the security will be sold for to the public.

DOWN

1. Date transaction is executed.

2. The increase in value of an asset. Sometimes called growth.

7. Anything that an individual or a corporation owns.

A. Trade date
B. Par value
C. Liquidity Risk
D. Capital Risk
E. Agency Debt
F. Amortization
G. Appreciation
H. Investment Banker
I. Asset
J. Code of Arbitrations

12. *Using the Across and Down clues, write the correct words in the numbered grid below.*

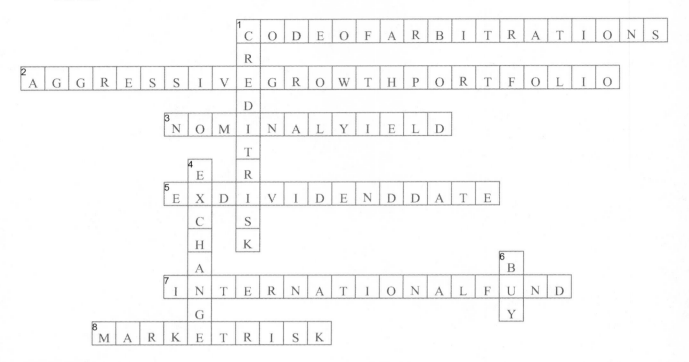

ACROSS

1. Provides a method of handling securities-related disputes or clearing controversies between members, public customers, clearing corporations or clearing banks.

2. Portfolio characterized by high turnover of holdings, attempts to cash in on higher-risk rapid capital appreciation situations.

3. Coupon, coupon rate, interest

5. The date the security trades without its dividends. In order to get a dividend the security needs to be purchased two days prior to the record date or before the ex-dividend date.

7. Common stocks from outside of the U.S.; Exposure to exchange rate risk and political (legistlative) risk, in addition to market risk.

8. Systematic risk

DOWN

1. Possibility that principal or interest will not be paid.

4. Switch

6. Own, Hold, Purchase, Long

A. Nominal yield
D. Aggressive Growth Portfolio
G. Market risk

B. International Fund
E. Buy
H. Code of Arbitrations

C. Exchange
F. Credit Risk
I. Ex dividend Date

13. *Using the Across and Down clues, write the correct words in the numbered grid below.*

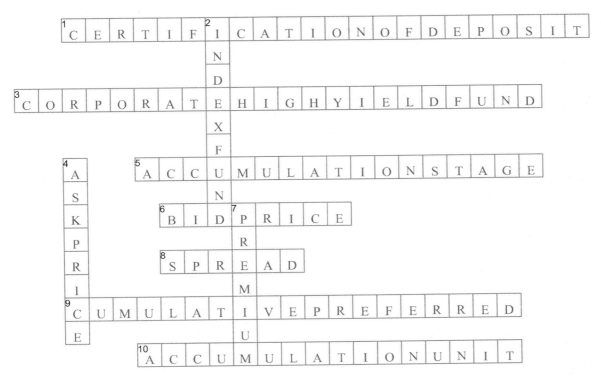

ACROSS

1. Issued by most commercial banks, representing bank borrowing for a short period of time.

3. Corporate bonds rate BB

5. The period during which contributions are made to an annuity account.

6. The price at which a dealer is willing to buy stock from an individual or another dealer.

8. Is the price difference the Market Maker is willing to buy the stock for, to the amount he

9. Has the right to receive skipped or missed dividends.

10. An accounting measure used to determine an annuitant's proportionate interest in the insurer's separate account during an annuity's accumulation (deposit) stage.

DOWN

2. Equity Category; Portfolio: common stock in same proportions as selected index.

4. The price at which the dealer is willing to sell the stock to an investor or another dealer.

7. Bonds that cost more than the face value.

A. Ask Price
D. Certification of Deposit
G. Bid Price
J. Accumulation Unit

B. Accumulation Stage
E. Corporate High Yield Fund
H. Index Fund

C. Spread
F. Cumulative Preferred
I. Premium

14. *Using the Across and Down clues, write the correct words in the numbered grid below.*

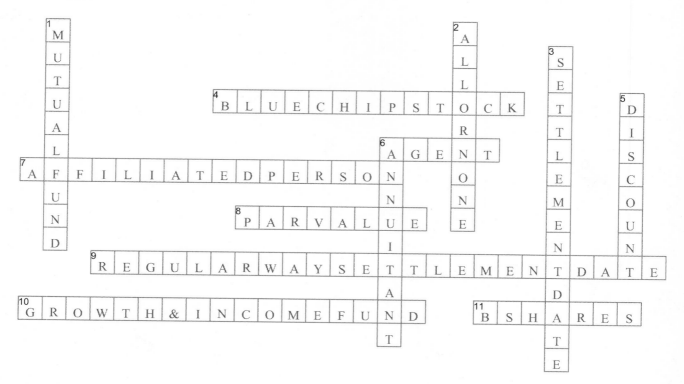

ACROSS

4. The stock of normally strong, well-established companies that have demonstrated their ability to pay dividends in good times and bad times.
6. An individual or a firm that effects securities transactions for the accounts of others.
7. Includes an investment adviser, officer, director, partner or employee of another person.
8. Face amount, principal
9. Refers to Corporate stocks
10. Mix of equities and bonds.
11. Bank End Load

DOWN

1. Open end management company.
2. States that the issuing company wants ALL (or nothing) the shares to be sold if not, the underwriting is cancelled.
3. Date transaction is completed and the seller pays buyer and the buyer receives the shares.
5. Bonds that are sold less then par value.
6. Person who receives an annuity contract's distribution.

A. Mutual Fund
D. Blue Chip Stock
G. Settlement date
J. Affiliated Person

B. Agent
E. Regular way Settlement Date
H. All or none
K. Annuitant

C. Growth & Income Fund
F. Par value
I. Discount
L. B shares

15. *Using the Across and Down clues, write the correct words in the numbered grid below.*

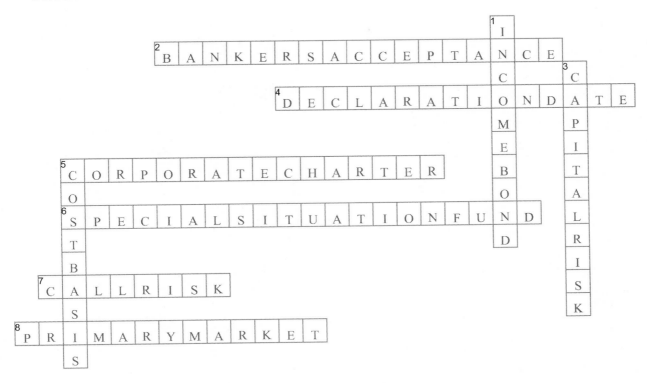

ACROSS

2. Essentially a letter of credit from a bank guaranteeing payment of a debt.

4. The date the Board of Directors announces intention of paying dividends.

5. Articles of Incorporation

6. Possible large gain if situation plays out as manager predicts; Depends on ability of manager to find special deals.

7. Bonds are more likely to be called when rates have dropped, forcing reinvestment of principal at lower rates.

8. New issue market, primary distribution, sold by prospectus only.

DOWN

1. Adjustment bond
3. Principal Risk
5. Money on which taxes have been paid. A return of cost basis is a return of capital and not subject to tax.

A. Declaration Date
D. Corporate Charter
G. Bankers Acceptance

B. Primary market
E. Capital Risk
H. Call Risk

C. Special Situation Fund
F. Income bond
I. Cost Basis

16. *Using the Across and Down clues, write the correct words in the numbered grid below.*

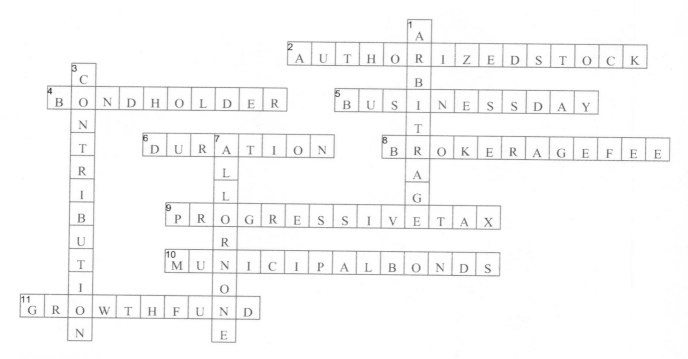

ACROSS

2. Authorized stock is the maximum number of shares a corporation may issue under the terms of its charter.

4. A creditor

5. A day the New York Stock Exchange is open for business (trading).

6. Measure of the bond price in relations to the time the bond end. Taking in consideration the interest-rates, time to maturity, and differences between the coupon rate and the yield to maturity.

8. Sales Charge, Sales Load

9. Graduated tax, income tax

10. Tax-free bonds

11. Common stock; capital appreciation; income not a consideration; subject to market fluctuations.

DOWN

1. The technique of buying and selling the same financial instrument in two different markets simultaneously to take advantage of a momentary price disparity.

3. Cost basis

7. States that the issuing company wants ALL (or nothing) the shares to be sold if not, the underwriting is cancelled.

A. Progressive tax
E. Municipal bonds
I. Growth Fund

B. Business Day
F. All or none
J. Brokerage fee

C. Duration
G. Arbitrage
K. Authorized Stock

D. Contribution
H. Bondholder

17. *Using the Across and Down clues, write the correct words in the numbered grid below.*

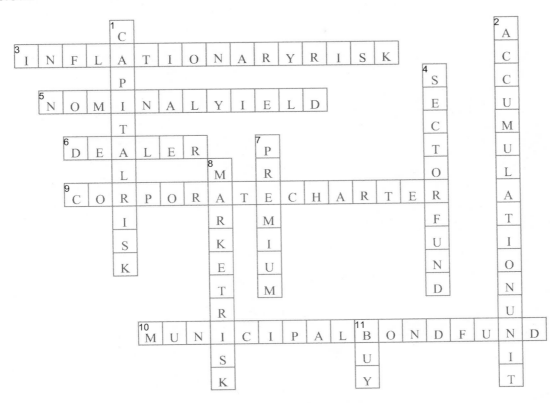

ACROSS

3. Rise in general level of prices reduces the value of fixed returns.

5. Yield stated on the bonds coupon.

6. Principal

9. Articles of Incorporation

10. Income that is free from federal, and possibly state income tax; higher the investor's tax bracket, the more beneficial the tax exemption; may have some default risk; interest rate risk.

DOWN

1. General term for possible loss of money invested. This risk is present in most securities.

2. An accounting measure used to determine an annuitant's proportionate interest in the insurer's separate account during an annuity's accumulation (deposit) stage.

4. Common stock from particular industry.

7. Bonds that cost more than the face value.

8. Possible loss of value due to a broad market decline. For equities, this risk is measured by a statistic called beta.

11. Own, Hold, Purchase, Long

A. Inflationary Risk
D. Market Risk
G. Corporate Charter
J. Capital Risk

B. Dealer
E. Municipal Bond Fund
H. Premium
K. Buy

C. Nominal yield
F. Sector Fund
I. Accumulation Unit

18. *Using the Across and Down clues, write the correct words in the numbered grid below.*

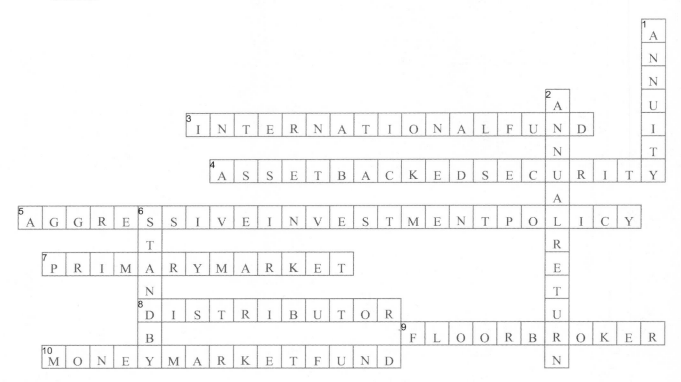

ACROSS

3. Common stocks from outside of the U.S.; Exposure to exchange rate risk and political (legistlative) risk, in addition to market risk.

4. A debt security backed by a loan, lease or receivables against assets other than real estate and mortgage-backed securities.

5. A policy concentrating on maximum return. Such a policy entails increased risks.

7. Where new issues of stock are issued. The only time when issuing companies make a profit on their shares.

8. Wholesaler, sponsor, underwriter

9. Buys stocks for its clients and for personal needs based on their listing price on the floor.

10. Cash equivalents such as T-bills, CDs, commercial paper, BAs; Preservation of Capital; attempts to maintain $1 NAV ; used to park funds while making investment decisions.

DOWN

1. A contract between an insurance company and an individual, generally guaranteeing lifetime income to the individual.

2. Holding period return

6. Allows the Underwriting firm to purchase any shares that the issuing company's shareholders have not bought and sell the shares themselves for a profit.

A. International Fund
D. Asset Backed Security
G. Floor Broker
J. Annual return

B. Primary Market
E. Aggressive Investment Policy
H. Standby

C. Distributor
F. Annuity
I. Money Market Fund

19. *Using the Across and Down clues, write the correct words in the numbered grid below.*

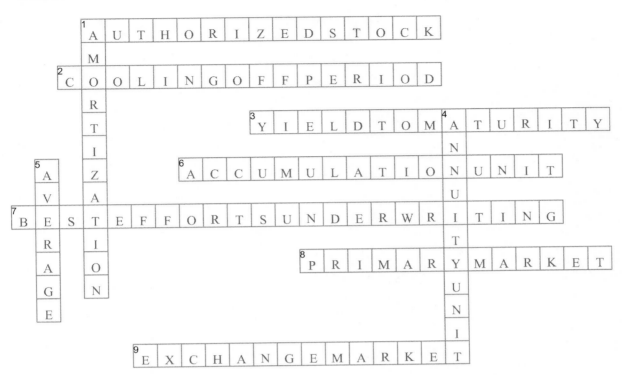

ACROSS

1. The number of shares of stock that a corporation may issue.

2. Traditionally, the 20-day period between the filing date of a registration statement and the effective date of the registration.

3. Calculation of a bonds total return if held until the end of its life (maturity).

6. An accounting measure used to determine an annuitant's proportionate interest in the insurer's separate account during an annuity's accumulation (deposit) stage.

7. Acting as an agent for the issuer, the underwriter puts forth his or her best efforts to sell as many shares as possible.

8. New issue market, primary distribution, sold by prospectus only.

9. Auction market

DOWN

1. Payment of a debt (principal) over a period of time in periodic installments.

4. An accounting measure used to determine the amount of each payment during an annuity's distribution stage.

5. A price at a midpoint among a number of prices. Technical analysts often use averages as market indicators.

A. Best Efforts Underwriting
D. Primary market
G. Accumulation Unit
J. Exchange market

B. Yield to maturity
E. Annuity Unit
H. Authorized Stock

C. Amortization
F. Cooling off Period
I. Average

20. *Using the Across and Down clues, write the correct words in the numbered grid below.*

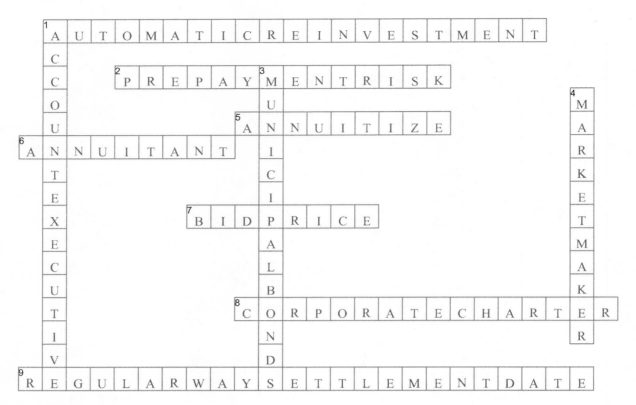

ACROSS

1. An option available to mutual fund shareholders whereby fund dividends and capital gains distributions are automatically reinvested back into the fund.

2. Fixed-Income Securities: Possibility that homeowners will prepay mortgages more quickly than expected when interest rates fall.

5. To change an annuity contract from the accumulation (pay-in) stage to the distribution (payout) stage.

6. Person who receives an annuity contract's distribution.

7. The price at which a dealer is willing to buy stock from an individual or another dealer.

8. Articles of Incorporation

9. Refers to Corporate stocks

DOWN

1. Registered Representative

3. Tax-free bonds

4. Broker-dealer firm primarily on the NASDAQ that opens bids and sells a particular security, taking on the risk of selling that security.

A. Annuitize
D. Municipal bonds
G. Regular way Settlement Date
J. Bid Price

B. Annuitant
E. Automatic Reinvestment
H. Corporate Charter

C. Prepayment Risk
F. Market Maker
I. Account Executive

21. *Using the Across and Down clues, write the correct words in the numbered grid below.*

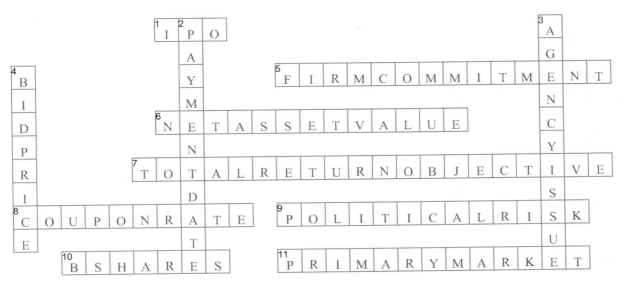

ACROSS

1. Primary Offering. New issues that are offered in the primary market and are sold to the public for the first time.

5. Bank buys issuing companies shares and sells them on the market for commission. Shares are not owned by the banks.

6. The price of a mutual fund. Calculates to company's funds minus liabilities divided by outstanding shares.

7. Investment objective for a combination of growth of capital and income, but less of each than investments that focus on just one of those objectives.

8. Nominal Yield

9. Changes in laws or rules may have negative impact on investments. The common wisdom is that political risk is high anytime Congress is in session.

10. Bank End Load

11. Where new issues of stock are issued. The only time when issuing companies make a profit on their shares.

DOWN

2. The date the company mails out the dividend.

3. A debt security issued by an authorized agency of the federal government.

4. The price at which a dealer is willing to buy stock from an individual or another dealer.

A. Total Return Objective
D. Bid Price
G. Payment date
J. Coupon Rate

B. Net Asset Value
E. B shares
H. Agency Issue
K. IPO

C. Primary Market
F. Political Risk
I. Firm Commitment

22. *Using the Across and Down clues, write the correct words in the numbered grid below.*

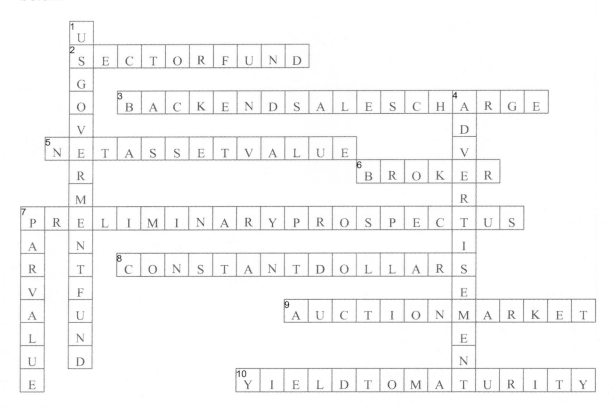

ACROSS

2. Common stock from particular industry.
3. Contingent deferred sales charge (CDSC)
5. The price of a mutual fund. Calculates to company's funds minus liabilities divided by outstanding shares.
6. An agent
7. Red Herring
8. Dollars adjusted to show the same purchasing power from one period to another. They are "indexed" for inflation.
9. A market in which buyers enter competitive bids and sellers enter competitive offers simultaneously.
10. Calculation of a bonds total return if held until the end of its life (maturity).

DOWN

1. T-bonds, T-notes, T-bills; Income with no credit risk; may be subject to interest rate risk; the longer average maturity of the portfolio the greater the interest rate risk
4. Any material designed for use by newspapers, magazines, radio, television, telephone, recordings or any other public medium to solicit business.
7. Face amount, principal

A. Preliminary prospectus
B. US Goverment Fund
C. Back end sales charge
D. Sector Fund
E. Advertisement
F. Broker
G. Net Asset Value
H. Constant dollars
I. Yield to maturity
J. Par value
K. Auction Market

23. *Using the Across and Down clues, write the correct words in the numbered grid below.*

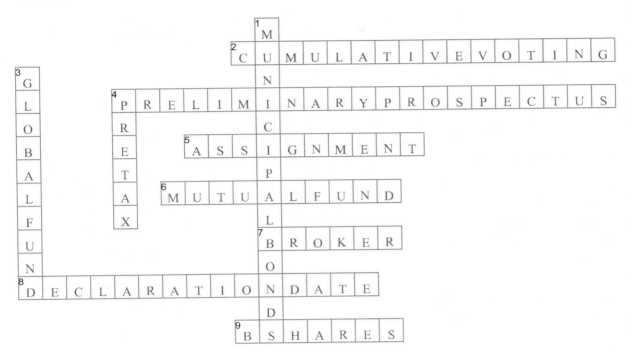

ACROSS

2. A type of shareholder voting in which the number of shares held is multiplied by the number of directors to be elected to determine the number of votes a shareholder may cast.

4. Red Herring

5. A document accompanying or part of a stock certificate that is signed by the person named on the certificate for the purpose of transferring the certificate's title to another person's name.

6. Open end management company.

7. The role of a brokerage firm when it acts as an agent for a customer and charges the customer a commission for its services.

8. The date on which the company declares an upcoming dividend.

9. Bank End Load

DOWN

1. Tax-free bonds

3. Common stock from inside and outside the U.S. Capital appreciation in whatever markets look attractive to manager.

4. Tax- deductible

A. Mutual Fund
D. Broker
G. B shares
J. Preliminary prospectus

B. Declaration Date
E. Global Fund
H. Assignment

C. Cumulative Voting
F. Pre-tax
I. Municipal bonds

24. *Using the Across and Down clues, write the correct words in the numbered grid below.*

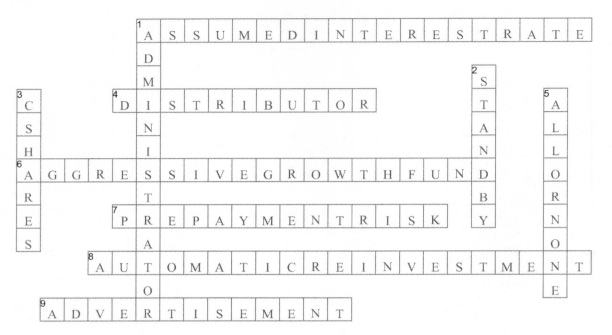

ACROSS

1. The net rate of investment return that must be credited to a variable life insurance policy to ensure that at all times the variable death benefit equals the amount of the death benefit.

4. Wholesaler, sponsor, underwriter

6. Small cap stocks; maximum capital appreciation; may employ short-term trading strategies; very volatile.

7. Fixed-Income Securities: Possibility that homeowners will prepay mortgages more quickly than expected when interest rates fall.

8. An option available to mutual fund shareholders whereby fund dividends and capital gains distributions are automatically reinvested back into the fund.

9. Any material designed for use by newspapers, magazines, radio, television, telephone, recordings or any other public medium to solicit business.

DOWN

1. A person authorized by a court of law to liquidate an intestate decedent's estate.

2. Allows the Underwriting firm to purchase any shares that the issuing company's shareholders have not bought and sell the shares themselves for a profit.

3. Level Load

5. A type of best efforts underwriting where the entire amount must be sold or the deal is called off.

A. C shares
D. Standby
G. Prepayment Risk
J. All or None

B. Aggressive Growth Fund
E. Advertisement
H. Assumed Interest Rate

C. Automatic Reinvestment
F. Administrator
I. Distributor

25. *Using the Across and Down clues, write the correct words in the numbered grid below.*

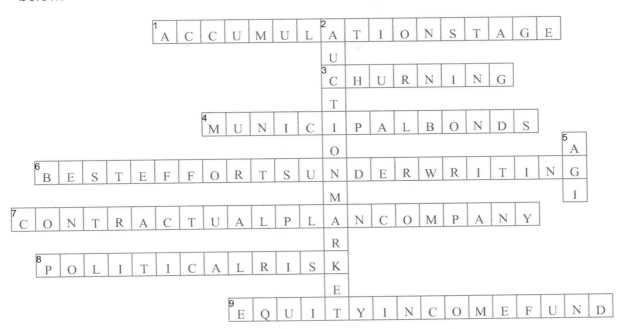

ACROSS

1. The period during which contributions are made to an annuity account.

3. Excessive trading in a customer's account. The registered representative ignores the objectives and interest of clients and seeks only to increase commissions.

4. Tax-free bonds

6. Acting as an agent for the issuer, the underwriter puts forth his or her best efforts to sell as many shares as possible.

7. A unit investment trust with which an investor may contact to buy mutual fund shares at fixed intervals over a fixed period of time.

8. Changes in laws or rules may have negative impact on investments. The common wisdom is that political risk is high anytime Congress is in session.

9. Dividend paying equities; safe, consistent income with secondary objective of growth; less volatile than other equity funds.

DOWN

2. A stock exchange where the securities are sold to the highest bidder.

5. Adjusted Gross Income. Earned income plus net passive income, portfolio income, and capital gains.

A. Municipal bonds
D. Contractual Plan Company
G. AGI

B. Churning
E. Best Efforts Underwriting
H. Accumulation Stage

C. Political Risk
F. Equity Income Fund
I. Auction Market

Multiple Choice

From the words provided for each clue, provide the letter of the word which best matches the clue.

1. ____ Has the right to receive skipped or missed dividends.
   A.convertible bond B.contractual plan company C.auction market D.cumulative preferred

2. ____ Tax-free bonds
   A.municipal bonds B.brokerage fee C.liquidity objective D.authorized stock

3. ____ The date the security trades without its dividends. In order to get a dividend the security needs to be purchased two days prior to the record date or before the ex-dividend date.
   A.call provisions B.floor broker C.market value D.ex dividend date

4. ____ Date transaction is executed.
   A.currency risk B.agency debt C.non-systematic risk D.trade date

5. ____ Any promotional material designed for use by newspapers, magazines, billboards, radio, television, telephone recordings or other public media.
   A.advertisement B.collateral trust bond C.authorized stock D.mutual fund

6. ____ Any material designed for use by newspapers, magazines, radio, television, telephone, recordings or any other public medium to solicit business.
   A.agency debt B.annuity unit C.automatic reinvestment D.advertisement

7. ____ Common stocks from outside of the U.S.; Exposure to exchange rate risk and political (legistlative) risk, in addition to market risk.
   A.broker B.balanced fund C.floor broker D.international fund

8. ____ Provides a method of handling securities-related disputes or clearing controversies between members, public customers, clearing corporations or clearing banks.
   A.c shares B.annuity unit C.non-systematic risk D.code of arbitrations

9. ____ General term for possible loss of money invested. This risk is present in most securities.
   A.authorized stock B.cost basis C.discount D.capital risk

10. ____ Investment objective for high-bracket investors facing a big tax bite on taxable investments may find tax-exempt vehicles produce a better after tax return.
    A.contractual plan company B.tax reduction objective C.balanced fund D.discount

11. ____ The increase in an asset's value.
    A.specialist B.appreciation C.investment income D.agi

12. ____ The sale of investment company shares in amounts just below the point at which the sales charge is reduced on quantity.
    A.c shares B.breakpoint sale C.asset backed security D.specialist

13. ____ Form of debt backed by stocks and or bonds of another corporation. The collateral is held by a trustee for safekeeping.
    A.liquidity objective B.agency issue C.accumulation stage D.collateral trust bond

14. ____ The date on which the company declares an upcoming dividend.
    A.agi B.auction market C.declaration date D.trade date

15. ____ A market in which buyers enter competitive bids and sellers enter competitive offers simultaneously.
    A.auction market B.contractual plan company C.code of arbitrations D.liquidity objective

16. ____ Mix of equities and bonds; growth with opportunity for income; portfolio mix usually under tighter constraints than growth & income fund.
A.balanced fund   B.all or none   C.agi   D.capital risk

17. ____ A type of mutual fund whose investment policy is to provide stable income with a minimum of capital risks.
A.bond fund   B.contractual plan company   C.bull market   D.appreciation

18. ____ A debt security backed by a loan, lease or receivables against assets other than real estate and mortgage-backed securities.
A.opportunity cost risk   B.asset backed security   C.coupon rate   D.currency risk

19. ____ An option available to mutual fund shareholders whereby fund dividends and capital gains distributions are automatically reinvested back into the fund.
A.property tax   B.accrued interest   C.combined annuity   D.automatic reinvestment

20. ____ The price at which the dealer is willing to sell the stock to an investor or another dealer.
A.ask price   B.common stock   C.sector fund   D.combined annuity

21. ____ Auctioneer of the stock, sets the opening bid, facilitates the trade between brokers and dealers, and makes sure the best bid for the stock is executed and sold.
A.declaration date   B.specialist   C.brokerage fee   D.call risk

22. ____ Selection risk, business risk
A.call risk   B.assumed interest rate   C.non-systematic risk   D.declaration date

23. ____ Control person, affiliate
A.insider   B.cumulative preferred   C.bull market   D.assumed interest rate

24. ____ Actual dollar amounts. Not adjusted for inflation.
A.specialist   B.bond   C.authorized stock   D.current dollars

25. ____ Changes in value of a currency versus another currency. Current owners of forign securities may see a negative impact if foreign currency weakens against their home currency.
A.currency risk   B.insider   C.all or none   D.assumed interest rate

26. ____ Rise in general level of prices reduces the value of fixed returns.
A.b shares   B.exchange   C.spread   D.inflationary risk

27. ____ Face amount, principal
A.municipal bonds   B.automatic reinvestment   C.growth & income fund   D.par value

28. ____ A type of mutual fund that at all times some portion of its investment assets in bonds and stocks, creating a balance between the two types of securities.
A.cumulative preferred   B.balanced fund   C.common stock   D.bond rating

29. ____ An individual or a firm that effects securities transactions for the accounts of others.
A.agency debt   B.agent   C.advertisement   D.distributor

30. ____ Is the price difference the Market Maker is willing to buy the stock for, to the amount he
A.spread   B.non-systematic risk   C.growth & income fund   D.coupon rate

31. ____ The date the Board of Directors announces intention of paying dividends.
A.convertible preferred stock   B.exchange   C.combined annuity   D.declaration date

32. ____ A debt security issued by an authorized agency of the federal government.
A.bankers acceptance   B.credit risk   C.tax reduction objective   D.agency issue

33. ____ An agent
A.aggressive growth fund   B.broker   C.agency debt   D.credit risk

34. ____ Allows the firm working for the issuing company to sell its shares the best way they can and are not responsible if shares are not sold.
A.best efforts   B.ask price   C.property tax   D.asked

35. ____ The quality of a bond issue as determined by independent bond rating services. AAA being of the highest quality.
A.balanced fund   B.firm commitment   C.bond rating   D.capital risk

36. ____ Front end sales charge, front end load
A.class a shares   B.convertible preferred stock   C.average   D.ask price

37. ____ Small cap stocks; maximum capital appreciation; may employ short-term trading strategies; very volatile.
A.firm commitment   B.aggressive growth fund   C.floor broker   D.credit risk

38. ____ Buys stocks for its clients and for personal needs based on their listing price on the floor.
A.floor broker   B.assumed interest rate   C.bond rating   D.brokerage fee

39. ____ Investment objective for investors that are willing and able to take considerable risks for the chance to hit a big financial home run.
A.speculation objective   B.special situation fund   C.convertible preferred stock   D.insider

40. ____ Possibility that principal or interest will not be paid.
A.declaration date   B.investment banker   C.balanced fund   D.credit risk

41. ____ Default risk
A.growth objective   B.corporate charter   C.credit risk   D.mutual fund

42. ____ This is the price an investor would pay when buying the security.
A.asked   B.liquidity objective   C.advertisement   D.authorized stock

43. ____ Loss of income or appreciation because an investment was NOT made.
A.opportunity cost risk   B.assignment   C.accumulation stage   D.b shares

44. ____ The price of a mutual fund. Calculates to company's funds minus liabilities divided by outstanding shares.
A.liquidity objective   B.net asset value   C.credit risk   D.accumulation stage

45. ____ Articles of Incorporation
A.auction market   B.declaration date   C.corporate charter   D.convertible preferred stock

46. ____ Level Load
A.yield to maturity   B.agency issue   C.investment banker   D.c shares

47. ____ Essentially a letter of credit from a bank guaranteeing payment of a debt.
A.current dollars   B.bankers acceptance   C.capital risk   D.annuitant

48. ____ The interest that has accumulated since the last interest payment up to, but not including, the settlement date, and that is added to a bond transaction's contract price.
A.accrued interest   B.assignment   C.non-systematic risk   D.authorized stock

49. ____ Nominal Yield
A.mutual fund   B.capital risk   C.coupon rate   D.class a shares

50. ____ The annuity contract holder.
A.annuitant   B.balanced fund   C.declaration date   D.credit risk

51. ____ This is a primary need for those who never know when they will need cash quickly.
A.current dollars   B.breakpoint   C.liquidity objective   D.currency risk

52. ____ Bank buys issuing companies shares and sells them on the market for commission. Shares are not owned by the banks.
A.firm commitment   B.common stock   C.political risk   D.convertible bond

53. ____ Authorized stock is the maximum number of shares a corporation may issue under the terms of its charter.
A.breakpoint   B.authorized stock   C.accrued interest   D.non-systematic risk

54. ____ interest & dividends
A.growth objective   B.investment income   C.insider   D.bankers acceptance

55. ____ Switch
A.exchange   B.growth objective   C.annual compliance review   D.class a shares

56. ____ Common stock from particular industry.
A.balanced fund   B.sector fund   C.average   D.ask price

57. ____ An accounting measure used to determine the amount of each payment during an annuity's distribution stage.
A.annuity unit   B.long   C.annuitant   D.credit risk

58. ____ Sales Charge, Sales Load
A.brokerage fee   B.authorized stock   C.international fund   D.breakpoint

59. ____ The period during which contributions are made to an annuity account.
A.floor broker   B.yield to maturity   C.accumulation stage   D.credit risk

60. ____ "New" stock
A.capital risk   B.corporate charter   C.balanced fund   D.authorized stock

61. ____ Calculation of a bonds total return if held until the end of its life (maturity).
A.yield to maturity   B.declaration date   C.code of arbitrations   D.convertible preferred stock

62. ____ Money on which taxes have been paid. A return of cost basis is a return of capital and not subject to tax.
A.net asset value   B.cost basis   C.class a shares   D.balanced fund

63. ____ Introduces new securities to the market, that advises the issuing company of the price the security will be sold for to the public.
A.floor broker   B.credit risk   C.all or none   D.investment banker

64. ____ The schedule of sales charge discounts offered by a mutual fund for lump sum or cumulative investments. Eligibility requirements must be disclosed in the prospectus.
A.annual compliance review   B.breakpoint   C.international fund   D.market value

65. ____ Adjusted Gross Income. Earned income plus net passive income, portfolio income, and capital gains.
A.auction market   B.asked   C.agi   D.ex dividend date

66. ____ Equity Category; Portfolio: common stock in same proportions as selected index.
A.all or none   B.current dollars   C.cumulative preferred   D.index fund

67. ___ A market in which prices of securities are moving higher or are expected to move higher.
A.bull market   B.agent   C.automatic reinvestment   D.balanced fund

68. ___ A base for illustrating payments from a variable annuity.
A.combined annuity   B.assumed interest rate   C.bond   D.agent

69. ___ An issuing corporation retains the privilege of recalling (redeeming) its issues of equity or debt.
A.call provisions   B.cumulative preferred   C.authorized stock   D.index fund

70. ___ An annuity combining the features of the fixed and variable annuities.
A.combined annuity   B.brokerage fee   C.floor broker   D.exchange

71. ___ Registered Representative
A.declaration date   B.political risk   C.automatic reinvestment   D.account executive

72. ___ Over the counter. A negotiated market.
A.otc   B.credit risk   C.advertisement   D.collateral trust bond

73. ___ Principal Risk
A.convertible bond   B.contractual plan company   C.discount   D.capital risk

74. ___ Mix of equities and bonds.
A.ex dividend date   B.discount   C.brokerage fee   D.growth & income fund

75. ___ Changes in laws or rules may have negative impact on investments. The common wisdom is that political risk is high anytime Congress is in session.
A.index fund   B.property tax   C.agency debt   D.political risk

76. ___ Bonds are more likely to be called when rates have dropped, forcing reinvestment of principal at lower rates.
A.yield to maturity   B.call risk   C.asked   D.asset backed security

77. ___ The basic stock issued by a corporation representing shares of ownership.
A.declaration date   B.convertible bond   C.common stock   D.speculation objective

78. ___ Represent the borrowing of money by a corporation or government.
A.political risk   B.corporate charter   C.bond   D.inflationary risk

79. ___ Often called "Indirect Debt."
A.special situation fund   B.investment income   C.agency debt   D.speculation objective

80. ___ Ability to quickly sell an investment at or near current market price. Regardless of type, more heavily traded securities are more liquid.
A.liquidity risk   B.opportunity cost risk   C.investment income   D.liquidity objective

81. ___ Bonds that cost more than the face value.
A.premium   B.cumulative preferred   C.call risk   D.spread

82. ___ Preferred stock that may be converted into common stock at the option of the holder.
A.market value   B.convertible preferred stock   C.contractual plan company   D.tax reduction objective

83. ___ Bonds that are sold less then par value.
A.agency debt   B.discount   C.aggressive growth fund   D.breakpoint

84. ___ A document accompanying or part of a stock certificate that is signed by the person named on the certificate for the purpose of transferring the certificate's title to another person's name.
A.assignment   B.ex dividend date   C.capital risk   D.agency issue

85. ___ Current bid and asking price of security.
A.advertisement   B.market value   C.account executive   D.bond fund

86. ___ Buy, bought, hold, or own
A.long   B.premium   C.annuitant   D.best efforts

87. ___ States that the issuing company wants ALL (or nothing) the shares to be sold if not, the underwriting is cancelled.
A.all or none   B.collateral trust bond   C.accrued interest   D.accumulation stage

88. ___ The number of shares of stock that a corporation may issue.
A.special situation fund   B.bull market   C.authorized stock   D.distributor

89. ___ Ad Valorem tax
A.property tax   B.credit risk   C.declaration date   D.credit risk

90. ___ A price at a midpoint among a number of prices. Technical analysts often use averages as market indicators.
A.average   B.cumulative preferred   C.growth objective   D.advertisement

91. ___ The accounting measure used to determine the amount of each payment to an annuitant during the pay-out period.
A.accumulation stage   B.annuitant   C.annuity unit   D.speculation objective

92. ___ A bond that may be exchanged for some other security of the issuer at the option of the holder. It is usually converted into common stock based upon a fixed conversion ratio.
A.convertible bond   B.growth & income fund   C.discount   D.agency issue

93. ___ A unit investment trust with which an investor may contact to buy mutual fund shares at fixed intervals over a fixed period of time.
A.trade date   B.contractual plan company   C.long   D.convertible preferred stock

94. ___ Investment objective for increase in invested capital, primarily generated through price appreciation. Equity securities (stocks) are usually used in pursuit of this goal.
A.convertible preferred stock   B.breakpoint   C.growth objective   D.annuity unit

95. ___ Income that is free from federal, and possibly state income tax; higher the investor's tax bracket, the more beneficial the tax exemption; may have some default risk; interest rate risk.
A.declaration date   B.municipal bond fund   C.mutual fund   D.property tax

96. ___ Bank End Load
A.account executive   B.convertible preferred stock   C.b shares   D.political risk

97. ___ Open end management company.
A.brokerage fee   B.capital risk   C.mutual fund   D.bull market

98. ___ The annual meeting that all registered representatives and principals must attend, the purpose of which is to review compliance issues.
A.credit risk   B.advertisement   C.market value   D.annual compliance review

99. ___ Wholesaler, sponsor, underwriter
A.distributor   B.investment banker   C.ex dividend date   D.call risk

100. ___ Possible large gain if situation plays out as manager predicts; Depends on ability of manager to find special deals.
A.special situation fund   B.investment income   C.corporate charter   D.ex dividend date

From the words provided for each clue, provide the letter of the word which best matches the clue.

101. ____ A contract between an insurance company and an individual, generally guaranteeing lifetime income to the individual.
A.credit risk   B.agency basis   C.annuity   D.common stock

102. ____ Auctioneer of the stock, sets the opening bid, facilitates the trade between brokers and dealers, and makes sure the best bid for the stock is executed and sold.
A.c shares   B.premium   C.contractual plan   D.specialist

103. ____ Any institution or an individual meeting minimum net worth requirements for the purchase of securities qualifying under the Regulation D registration exemption.
A.equity income fund   B.accredited investor   C.bid price   D.interest rate risk

104. ____ Equity Category; Portfolio: common stock in same proportions as selected index.
A.brokerage fee   B.index fund   C.constant dollars   D.conduit theory

105. ____ The price at which the dealer is willing to sell the stock to an investor or another dealer.
A.total return objective   B.investment income   C.ask price   D.long

106. ____ Default risk
A.american depository receipt   B.timing risk   C.annual compliance review   D.credit risk

107. ____ Tax- deductible
A.bid   B.pre-tax   C.dealer   D.ask

108. ____ Preferred stock that may be converted into common stock at the option of the holder.
A.timing risk   B.annual compliance review   C.all or none   D.convertible preferred stock

109. ____ Date where the BOD checks if a shareholder is listed with the company, so they can get paid their dividends.
A.call option   B.international fund   C.record date   D.exchange market

110. ____ Form of debt backed by stocks and or bonds of another corporation. The collateral is held by a trustee for safekeeping.
A.ex dividend date   B.collateral trust bond   C.annuity unit   D.all or none

111. ____ Selection risk, business risk
A.outstanding shares   B.non-systematic risk   C.conduit theory   D.contractual plan company

112. ____ To change an annuity contract from the accumulation (pay-in) stage to the distribution (payout) stage.
A.annuitize   B.insider   C.equity income fund   D.mutual fund family

113. ____ The price a Market Maker will pay for a security; it's the price an investor would receive if he or she sold the security.
A.c shares   B.bid   C.agency debt   D.currency risk

114. ____ Red Herring
A.preliminary prospectus   B.insider   C.dealer   D.property tax

115. ____ Buy, bought, hold, or own
A.long   B.asset   C.annuity unit   D.call price

116. ____ Possible loss of value due to a broad market decline. For equities, this risk is measured by a statistic called beta.
A.index fund   B.payment date   C.liquidity objective   D.market risk

117. ____ A bond that may be exchanged for some other security of the issuer at the option of the holder. It is usually converted into common stock based upon a fixed conversion ratio.
A.exchange market B.contractual plan C.convertible bond D.agency debt

118. ____ The price of a mutual fund. Calculates to company's funds minus liabilities divided by outstanding shares.
A.net asset value B.firm commitment C.market risk D.convertible preferred stock

119. ____ Ad Valorem tax
A.cumulative voting B.property tax C.collateral trust bond D.conduit theory

120. ____ Often called "Indirect Debt."
A.equity income fund B.market risk C.ask price D.agency debt

121. ____ Dividend paying equities; safe, consistent income with secondary objective of growth; less volatile than other equity funds.
A.income objective B.equity income fund C.equity income fund D.timing risk

122. ____ Control person, affiliate
A.annuitize B.non-systematic risk C.insider D.tax reduction objective

123. ____ Growth and income fund
A.constant dollars B.american depository receipt C.equity income fund D.prepayment risk

124. ____ A type of best efforts underwriting where the entire amount must be sold or the deal is called off.
A.exchange market B.tax reduction objective C.current dollars D.all or none

125. ____ An accounting measure used to determine the amount of each payment during an annuity's distribution stage.
A.auction market B.current yield C.assumed interest rate D.annuity unit

126. ____ The price paid for callable preferred stock or bonds redeemed by the issuer prior to maturity of the issue because interest rates have fallen.
A.aggressive growth fund B.call price C.current yield D.us goverment fund

127. ____ Actual dollar amounts. Not adjusted for inflation.
A.exchange market B.current dollars C.exchange D.best efforts

128. ____ Possible large gain if situation plays out as manager predicts; Depends on ability of manager to find special deals.
A.convertible bond B.call option C.special situation fund D.c shares

129. ____ Dollars adjusted to show the same purchasing power from one period to another. They are "indexed" for inflation.
A.constant dollars B.blue chip stock C.bid D.outstanding shares

130. ____ Contingent deferred sales charge (CDSC)
A.credit risk B.amt C.back end sales charge D.business day

131. ____ Payment of a debt (principal) over a period of time in periodic installments.
A.common stock B.annuitize C.municipal bonds D.amortization

132. ____ The date the security trades without its dividends. In order to get a dividend the security needs to be purchased two days prior to the record date or before the ex-dividend date.
A.timing risk B.american depository receipt C.ex dividend date D.liquidity objective

133. ____ American Depository Shares
A.long B.keogh plan C.contractual plan company D.american depository receipt

134. ___ Has the right to receive skipped or missed dividends.
A.balanced fund   B.business day   C.cumulative preferred   D.aggressive growth fund

135. ___ Portfolio characterized by high turnover of holdings, attempts to cash in on higher-risk rapid capital appreciation situations.
A.market risk   B.annuity   C.record date   D.aggressive growth portfolio

136. ___ Alternative Minimum Tax. The requirement to add the income from tax preference items to income above an indexed level. A method to insure that wealthy persons and corporations pay at least some tax.
A.bid   B.corporate high yield fund   C.amt   D.accumulation stage

137. ___ The date the company mails out the dividend.
A.preliminary prospectus   B.timing risk   C.payment date   D.equity income fund

138. ___ Sales Charge, Sales Load
A.bid price   B.exchange   C.corporate high yield fund   D.brokerage fee

139. ___ Present yield the buyer would receive when purchasing the bond. Calculated by dividing Annual Interest rates to Market Price.
A.outstanding shares   B.preliminary prospectus   C.accumulation unit   D.current yield

140. ___ An agency Transaction
A.duration   B.agency basis   C.asset   D.convertible bond

141. ___ Cost basis
A.contribution   B.special situation fund   C.distributor   D.keogh plan

142. ___ Also called period payment plans.
A.currency risk   B.outstanding shares   C.contractual plan   D.total return objective

143. ___ Possibility that increase in general level of interest rates will drive down prices of existing fixed-income investments.
A.amt   B.interest rate risk   C.appreciation   D.liquidity objective

144. ___ Registered Representative
A.conduit theory   B.total return objective   C.account executive   D.timing risk

145. ___ The period during which contributions are made to an annuity account.
A.annuitize   B.firm commitment   C.duration   D.accumulation stage

146. ___ The price at which a dealer is willing to buy stock from an individual or another dealer.
A.call option   B.record date   C.auction market   D.bid price

147. ___ Allows the firm working for the issuing company to sell its shares the best way they can and are not responsible if shares are not sold.
A.best efforts   B.c shares   C.interest rate risk   D.constant dollars

148. ___ Mix of equities and bonds; growth with opportunity for income; portfolio mix usually under tighter constraints than growth & income fund.
A.record date   B.balanced fund   C.bid   D.total return objective

149. ___ Investment objective for investors that are willing and able to take considerable risks for the chance to hit a big financial home run.
A.authorized stock   B.appreciation   C.cumulative preferred   D.speculation objective

150. ____ Investment objective for high-bracket investors facing a big tax bite on taxable investments may find tax-exempt vehicles produce a better after tax return.
A.tax reduction objective   B.current yield   C.exchange   D.aggressive growth portfolio

151. ____ Investment objective for a combination of growth of capital and income, but less of each than investments that focus on just one of those objectives.
A.common stock   B.convertible bond   C.liquidity objective   D.total return objective

152. ____ Excessive trading in a customer's account. The registered representative ignores the objectives and interest of clients and seeks only to increase commissions.
A.tax reduction objective   B.payment date   C.churning   D.debenture

153. ____ Common stocks from outside of the U.S.; Exposure to exchange rate risk and political (legistlative) risk, in addition to market risk.
A.account executive   B.market risk   C.international fund   D.total return objective

154. ____ Cash equivalents such as T-bills, CDs, commercial paper, BAs; Preservation of Capital; attempts to maintain $1 NAV ; used to park funds while making investment decisions.
A.b shares   B.asset   C.money market fund   D.corporate high yield fund

155. ____ Tax-free bonds
A.collateral trust bond   B.convertible bond   C.outstanding shares   D.municipal bonds

156. ____ unsecured Bond backed only by the good faith of the corporation. Repayment of the debt is based on the company's promise to repay.
A.income objective   B.contractual plan   C.cumulative preferred   D.debenture

157. ____ Fixed-Income Securities: Possibility that homeowners will prepay mortgages more quickly than expected when interest rates fall.
A.call option   B.specialist   C.prepayment risk   D.business day

158. ____ Any material designed for use by newspapers, magazines, radio, television, telephone, recordings or any other public medium to solicit business.
A.tax reduction objective   B.best efforts   C.advertisement   D.prepayment risk

159. ____ Calculation of a bonds total return if held until the end of its life (maturity).
A.agency debt   B.cumulative preferred   C.contractual plan   D.yield to maturity

160. ____ Switch
A.cumulative voting   B.exchange   C.firm commitment   D.conduit theory

161. ____ An option to buy a specified number of shares of stock at a definite price within a specified period of time. See put option.
A.payment date   B.call option   C.bankers acceptance   D.contractual plan company

162. ____ An accounting measure used to determine an annuitant's proportionate interest in the insurer's separate account during an annuity's accumulation (deposit) stage.
A.duration   B.cumulative preferred   C.accumulation unit   D.collateral trust bond

163. ____ Auction market
A.accumulation unit   B.prepayment risk   C.amortization   D.exchange market

164. ____ Essentially a letter of credit from a bank guaranteeing payment of a debt.
A.collateral trust bond   B.keogh plan   C.annuity unit   D.bankers acceptance

165. ____ A day the New York Stock Exchange is open for business (trading).
A.ask price   B.business day   C.interest rate risk   D.yield to maturity

166. ___ Small cap stocks; maximum capital appreciation; may employ short-term trading strategies; very volatile.
A.b shares   B.aggressive growth portfolio   C.contribution   D.aggressive growth fund

167. ___ Bonds that cost more than the face value.
A.american depository receipt   B.annuity   C.assumed interest rate   D.premium

168. ___ A stock exchange where the securities are sold to the highest bidder.
A.auction market   B.asset   C.blue chip stock   D.american depository receipt

169. ___ An indication of willingness by a trader or dealer to sell a security or a commodity.
A.ask   B.exchange   C.speculation objective   D.american depository receipt

170. ___ Corporate bonds rate BB
A.preliminary prospectus   B.market risk   C.net asset value   D.corporate high yield fund

171. ___ Changes in value of a currency versus another currency. Current owners of forign securities may see a negative impact if foreign currency weakens against their home currency.
A.debenture   B.amt   C.advertisement   D.currency risk

172. ___ The yield of the security when bought or sold prior to maturity in the secondary market. Current yield relates current income to the security's current price.
A.cumulative preferred   B.accredited investor   C.exchange market   D.current yield

173. ___ Shares held by the public
A.b shares   B.current yield   C.outstanding shares   D.money market fund

174. ___ Any promotional material designed for use by newspapers, magazines, billboards, radio, television, telephone recordings or other public media.
A.advertisement   B.cumulative voting   C.yield to maturity   D.interest rate risk

175. ___ The increase in an asset's value.
A.duration   B.distributor   C.current yield   D.appreciation

176. ___ A unit investment trust with which an investor may contact to buy mutual fund shares at fixed intervals over a fixed period of time.
A.annual compliance review   B.preliminary prospectus   C.contractual plan company   D.equity income fund

177. ___ A type of shareholder voting in which the number of shares held is multiplied by the number of directors to be elected to determine the number of votes a shareholder may cast.
A.equity income fund   B.constant dollars   C.cumulative voting   D.convertible preferred stock

178. ___ Anything that an individual or a corporation owns.
A.keogh plan   B.contribution   C.asset   D.account executive

179. ___ The basic stock issued by a corporation representing shares of ownership.
A.yield to maturity   B.payment date   C.firm commitment   D.common stock

180. ___ T-bonds, T-notes, T-bills; Income with no credit risk; may be subject to interest rate risk; the longer average maturity of the portfolio the greater the interest rate risk
A.cumulative voting   B.appreciation   C.us goverment fund   D.amortization

181. ___ Bank buys issuing companies shares and sells them on the market for commission. Shares are not owned by the banks.
A.firm commitment   B.long   C.account executive   D.total return objective

182. ____ Family of funds, mutual fund complex
A.payment date   B.advertisement   C.mutual fund family   D.accumulation stage

183. ____ Level Load
A.firm commitment   B.ask   C.c shares   D.annuity unit

184. ____ interest & dividends
A.b shares   B.mutual fund family   C.accredited investor   D.investment income

185. ____ The number of shares of stock that a corporation may issue.
A.authorized stock   B.specialist   C.income objective   D.payment date

186. ____ States that the issuing company wants ALL (or nothing) the shares to be sold if not, the underwriting is cancelled.
A.annuity unit   B.all or none   C.common stock   D.all or none

187. ____ A form of business organization in which the total worth of the organization is divided into shares of stock.
A.contribution   B.corporation   C.bid price   D.collateral trust bond

188. ____ A theory behind Subchapter M under which distributions to shareholders are not taxed to the investment company.
A.liquidity objective   B.credit risk   C.conduit theory   D.advertisement

189. ____ One who deals in securities as a principal, buying and selling for his own account.
A.assumed interest rate   B.dealer   C.exchange market   D.amortization

190. ____ Investment objective for regular production of cash from investments, through dividend or interest payments. Bonds and preferred stocks are often used to produce income.
A.current dollars   B.income objective   C.insider   D.contractual plan company

191. ____ The annual meeting that all registered representatives and principals must attend, the purpose of which is to review compliance issues.
A.annual compliance review   B.keogh plan   C.equity income fund   D.business day

192. ____ Wholesaler, sponsor, underwriter
A.account executive   B.american depository receipt   C.distributor   D.money market fund

193. ____ An HR-10 retirement Plan
A.money market fund   B.keogh plan   C.debenture   D.preliminary prospectus

194. ____ The annuity contract holder.
A.cumulative preferred   B.annuitant   C.premium   D.call price

195. ____ A base for illustrating payments from a variable annuity.
A.current yield   B.current dollars   C.equity income fund   D.assumed interest rate

196. ____ The stock of normally strong, well-established companies that have demonstrated their ability to pay dividends in good times and bad times.
A.blue chip stock   B.money market fund   C.annuitize   D.prepayment risk

197. ____ Investing in a specific security at an inopportune time. Dollar cost averaging is used to avoid this risk.
A.timing risk   B.advertisement   C.income objective   D.us goverment fund

198. ____ This is a primary need for those who never know when they will need cash quickly.
A.liquidity objective   B.auction market   C.keogh plan   D.constant dollars

199. ____ Measure of the bond price in relations to the time the bond end. Taking in consideration the interest-rates, time to maturity, and differences between the coupon rate and the yield to maturity.
A.brokerage fee   B.special situation fund   C.duration   D.balanced fund

200. ____ Bank End Load
A.bankers acceptance   B.b shares   C.money market fund   D.credit risk

From the words provided for each clue, provide the letter of the word which best matches the clue.

1. D   Has the right to receive skipped or missed dividends.
   A.convertible bond   B.contractual plan company   C.auction market   D.cumulative preferred

2. A   Tax-free bonds
   A.municipal bonds   B.brokerage fee   C.liquidity objective   D.authorized stock

3. D   The date the security trades without its dividends. In order to get a dividend the security needs to be purchased two days prior to the record date or before the ex-dividend date.
   A.call provisions   B.floor broker   C.market value   D.ex dividend date

4. D   Date transaction is executed.
   A.currency risk   B.agency debt   C.non-systematic risk   D.trade date

5. A   Any promotional material designed for use by newspapers, magazines, billboards, radio, television, telephone recordings or other public media.
   A.advertisement   B.collateral trust bond   C.authorized stock   D.mutual fund

6. D   Any material designed for use by newspapers, magazines, radio, television, telephone, recordings or any other public medium to solicit business.
   A.agency debt   B.annuity unit   C.automatic reinvestment   D.advertisement

7. D   Common stocks from outside of the U.S.; Exposure to exchange rate risk and political (legistlative) risk, in addition to market risk.
   A.broker   B.balanced fund   C.floor broker   D.international fund

8. D   Provides a method of handling securities-related disputes or clearing controversies between members, public customers, clearing corporations or clearing banks.
   A.c shares   B.annuity unit   C.non-systematic risk   D.code of arbitrations

9. D   General term for possible loss of money invested. This risk is present in most securities.
   A.authorized stock   B.cost basis   C.discount   D.capital risk

10. B   Investment objective for high-bracket investors facing a big tax bite on taxable investments may find tax-exempt vehicles produce a better after tax return.
    A.contractual plan company   B.tax reduction objective   C.balanced fund   D.discount

11. B   The increase in an asset's value.
    A.specialist   B.appreciation   C.investment income   D.agi

12. B   The sale of investment company shares in amounts just below the point at which the sales charge is reduced on quantity.
    A.c shares   B.breakpoint sale   C.asset backed security   D.specialist

13. D   Form of debt backed by stocks and or bonds of another corporation. The collateral is held by a trustee for safekeeping.
    A.liquidity objective   B.agency issue   C.accumulation stage   D.collateral trust bond

14. C   The date on which the company declares an upcoming dividend.
    A.agi   B.auction market   C.declaration date   D.trade date

15. A   A market in which buyers enter competitive bids and sellers enter competitive offers simultaneously.
    A.auction market   B.contractual plan company   C.code of arbitrations   D.liquidity objective

16. A   Mix of equities and bonds; growth with opportunity for income; portfolio mix usually under tighter constraints than growth & income fund.
A.balanced fund   B.all or none   C.agi   D.capital risk

17. A   A type of mutual fund whose investment policy is to provide stable income with a minimum of capital risks.
A.bond fund   B.contractual plan company   C.bull market   D.appreciation

18. B   A debt security backed by a loan, lease or receivables against assets other than real estate and mortgage-backed securities.
A.opportunity cost risk   B.asset backed security   C.coupon rate   D.currency risk

19. D   An option available to mutual fund shareholders whereby fund dividends and capital gains distributions are automatically reinvested back into the fund.
A.property tax   B.accrued interest   C.combined annuity   D.automatic reinvestment

20. A   The price at which the dealer is willing to sell the stock to an investor or another dealer.
A.ask price   B.common stock   C.sector fund   D.combined annuity

21. B   Auctioneer of the stock, sets the opening bid, facilitates the trade between brokers and dealers, and makes sure the best bid for the stock is executed and sold.
A.declaration date   B.specialist   C.brokerage fee   D.call risk

22. C   Selection risk, business risk
A.call risk   B.assumed interest rate   C.non-systematic risk   D.declaration date

23. A   Control person, affiliate
A.insider   B.cumulative preferred   C.bull market   D.assumed interest rate

24. D   Actual dollar amounts. Not adjusted for inflation.
A.specialist   B.bond   C.authorized stock   D.current dollars

25. A   Changes in value of a currency versus another currency. Current owners of forign securities may see a negative impact if foreign currency weakens against their home currency.
A.currency risk   B.insider   C.all or none   D.assumed interest rate

26. D   Rise in general level of prices reduces the value of fixed returns.
A.b shares   B.exchange   C.spread   D.inflationary risk

27. D   Face amount, principal
A.municipal bonds   B.automatic reinvestment   C.growth & income fund   D.par value

28. B   A type of mutual fund that at all times some portion of its investment assets in bonds and stocks, creating a balance between the two types of securities.
A.cumulative preferred   B.balanced fund   C.common stock   D.bond rating

29. B   An individual or a firm that effects securities transactions for the accounts of others.
A.agency debt   B.agent   C.advertisement   D.distributor

30. A   Is the price difference the Market Maker is willing to buy the stock for, to the amount he
A.spread   B.non-systematic risk   C.growth & income fund   D.coupon rate

31. D   The date the Board of Directors announces intention of paying dividends.
A.convertible preferred stock   B.exchange   C.combined annuity   D.declaration date

32. D   A debt security issued by an authorized agency of the federal government.
A.bankers acceptance   B.credit risk   C.tax reduction objective   D.agency issue

33. B   An agent
A.aggressive growth fund   B.broker   C.agency debt   D.credit risk

34. A   Allows the firm working for the issuing company to sell its shares the best way they can and are not responsible if shares are not sold.
A.best efforts   B.ask price   C.property tax   D.asked

35. C   The quality of a bond issue as determined by independent bond rating services. AAA being of the highest quality.
A.balanced fund   B.firm commitment   C.bond rating   D.capital risk

36. A   Front end sales charge, front end load
A.class a shares   B.convertible preferred stock   C.average   D.ask price

37. B   Small cap stocks; maximum capital appreciation; may employ short-term trading strategies; very volatile.
A.firm commitment   B.aggressive growth fund   C.floor broker   D.credit risk

38. A   Buys stocks for its clients and for personal needs based on their listing price on the floor.
A.floor broker   B.assumed interest rate   C.bond rating   D.brokerage fee

39. A   Investment objective for investors that are willing and able to take considerable risks for the chance to hit a big financial home run.
A.speculation objective   B.special situation fund   C.convertible preferred stock   D.insider

40. D   Possibility that principal or interest will not be paid.
A.declaration date   B.investment banker   C.balanced fund   D.credit risk

41. C   Default risk
A.growth objective   B.corporate charter   C.credit risk   D.mutual fund

42. A   This is the price an investor would pay when buying the security.
A.asked   B.liquidity objective   C.advertisement   D.authorized stock

43. A   Loss of income or appreciation because an investment was NOT made.
A.opportunity cost risk   B.assignment   C.accumulation stage   D.b shares

44. B   The price of a mutual fund. Calculates to company's funds minus liabilities divided by outstanding shares.
A.liquidity objective   B.net asset value   C.credit risk   D.accumulation stage

45. C   Articles of Incorporation
A.auction market   B.declaration date   C.corporate charter   D.convertible preferred stock

46. D   Level Load
A.yield to maturity   B.agency issue   C.investment banker   D.c shares

47. B   Essentially a letter of credit from a bank guaranteeing payment of a debt.
A.current dollars   B.bankers acceptance   C.capital risk   D.annuitant

48. A   The interest that has accumulated since the last interest payment up to, but not including, the settlement date, and that is added to a bond transaction's contract price.
A.accrued interest   B.assignment   C.non-systematic risk   D.authorized stock

49. C   Nominal Yield
A.mutual fund   B.capital risk   C.coupon rate   D.class a shares

50. A   The annuity contract holder.
A.annuitant   B.balanced fund   C.declaration date   D.credit risk

51. C   This is a primary need for those who never know when they will need cash quickly.
A.current dollars   B.breakpoint   C.liquidity objective   D.currency risk

52. A   Bank buys issuing companies shares and sells them on the market for commission. Shares are not owned by the banks.
A.firm commitment   B.common stock   C.political risk   D.convertible bond

53. B   Authorized stock is the maximum number of shares a corporation may issue under the terms of its charter.
A.breakpoint   B.authorized stock   C.accrued interest   D.non-systematic risk

54. B   interest & dividends
A.growth objective   B.investment income   C.insider   D.bankers acceptance

55. A   Switch
A.exchange   B.growth objective   C.annual compliance review   D.class a shares

56. B   Common stock from particular industry.
A.balanced fund   B.sector fund   C.average   D.ask price

57. A   An accounting measure used to determine the amount of each payment during an annuity's distribution stage.
A.annuity unit   B.long   C.annuitant   D.credit risk

58. A   Sales Charge, Sales Load
A.brokerage fee   B.authorized stock   C.international fund   D.breakpoint

59. C   The period during which contributions are made to an annuity account.
A.floor broker   B.yield to maturity   C.accumulation stage   D.credit risk

60. D   "New" stock
A.capital risk   B.corporate charter   C.balanced fund   D.authorized stock

61. A   Calculation of a bonds total return if held until the end of its life (maturity).
A.yield to maturity   B.declaration date   C.code of arbitrations   D.convertible preferred stock

62. B   Money on which taxes have been paid. A return of cost basis is a return of capital and not subject to tax.
A.net asset value   B.cost basis   C.class a shares   D.balanced fund

63. D   Introduces new securities to the market, that advises the issuing company of the price the security will be sold for to the public.
A.floor broker   B.credit risk   C.all or none   D.investment banker

64. B   The schedule of sales charge discounts offered by a mutual fund for lump sum or cumulative investments. Eligibility requirements must be disclosed in the prospectus.
A.annual compliance review   B.breakpoint   C.international fund   D.market value

65. C   Adjusted Gross Income. Earned income plus net passive income, portfolio income, and capital gains.
A.auction market   B.asked   C.agi   D.ex dividend date

66. D   Equity Category; Portfolio: common stock in same proportions as selected index.
A.all or none   B.current dollars   C.cumulative preferred   D.index fund

67. A   A market in which prices of securities are moving higher or are expected to move higher.
     A.bull market B.agent C.automatic reinvestment D.balanced fund

68. B   A base for illustrating payments from a variable annuity.
     A.combined annuity B.assumed interest rate C.bond D.agent

69. A   An issuing corporation retains the privilege of recalling (redeeming) its issues of equity or debt.
     A.call provisions B.cumulative preferred C.authorized stock D.index fund

70. A   An annuity combining the features of the fixed and variable annuities.
     A.combined annuity B.brokerage fee C.floor broker D.exchange

71. D   Registered Representative
     A.declaration date B.political risk C.automatic reinvestment D.account executive

72. A   Over the counter. A negotiated market.
     A.otc B.credit risk C.advertisement D.collateral trust bond

73. D   Principal Risk
     A.convertible bond B.contractual plan company C.discount D.capital risk

74. D   Mix of equities and bonds.
     A.ex dividend date B.discount C.brokerage fee D.growth & income fund

75. D   Changes in laws or rules may have negative impact on investments. The common wisdom is that political risk is high anytime Congress is in session.
     A.index fund B.property tax C.agency debt D.political risk

76. B   Bonds are more likely to be called when rates have dropped, forcing reinvestment of principal at lower rates.
     A.yield to maturity B.call risk C.asked D.asset backed security

77. C   The basic stock issued by a corporation representing shares of ownership.
     A.declaration date B.convertible bond C.common stock D.speculation objective

78. C   Represent the borrowing of money by a corporation or government.
     A.political risk B.corporate charter C.bond D.inflationary risk

79. C   Often called "Indirect Debt."
     A.special situation fund B.investment income C.agency debt D.speculation objective

80. A   Ability to quickly sell an investment at or near current market price. Regardless of type, more heavily traded securities are more liquid.
     A.liquidity risk B.opportunity cost risk C.investment income D.liquidity objective

81. A   Bonds that cost more than the face value.
     A.premium B.cumulative preferred C.call risk D.spread

82. B   Preferred stock that may be converted into common stock at the option of the holder.
     A.market value B.convertible preferred stock C.contractual plan company D.tax reduction objective

83. B   Bonds that are sold less then par value.
     A.agency debt B.discount C.aggressive growth fund D.breakpoint

84. A   A document accompanying or part of a stock certificate that is signed by the person named on the certificate for the purpose of transferring the certificate's title to another person's name.
     A.assignment B.ex dividend date C.capital risk D.agency issue

85. B Current bid and asking price of security.
    A.advertisement   B.market value   C.account executive   D.bond fund

86. A Buy, bought, hold, or own
    A.long   B.premium   C.annuitant   D.best efforts

87. A States that the issuing company wants ALL (or nothing) the shares to be sold if not, the
    underwriting is cancelled.
    A.all or none   B.collateral trust bond   C.accrued interest   D.accumulation stage

88. C The number of shares of stock that a corporation may issue.
    A.special situation fund   B.bull market   C.authorized stock   D.distributor

89. A Ad Valorem tax
    A.property tax   B.credit risk   C.declaration date   D.credit risk

90. A A price at a midpoint among a number of prices. Technical analysts often use averages as market
    indicators.
    A.average   B.cumulative preferred   C.growth objective   D.advertisement

91. C The accounting measure used to determine the amount of each payment to an annuitant during
    the pay-out period.
    A.accumulation stage   B.annuitant   C.annuity unit   D.speculation objective

92. A A bond that may be exchanged for some other security of the issuer at the option of the holder. It is
    usually converted into common stock based upon a fixed conversion ratio.
    A.convertible bond   B.growth & income fund   C.discount   D.agency issue

93. B A unit investment trust with which an investor may contact to buy mutual fund shares at fixed
    intervals over a fixed period of time.
    A.trade date   B.contractual plan company   C.long   D.convertible preferred stock

94. C Investment objective for increase in invested capital, primarily generated through price
    appreciation. Equity securities (stocks) are usually used in pursuit of this goal.
    A.convertible preferred stock   B.breakpoint   C.growth objective   D.annuity unit

95. B Income that is free from federal, and possibly state income tax; higher the investor's tax bracket,
    the more beneficial the tax exemption; may have some default risk; interest rate risk.
    A.declaration date   B.municipal bond fund   C.mutual fund   D.property tax

96. C Bank End Load
    A.account executive   B.convertible preferred stock   C.b shares   D.political risk

97. C Open end management company.
    A.brokerage fee   B.capital risk   C.mutual fund   D.bull market

98. D The annual meeting that all registered representatives and principals must attend, the purpose of
    which is to review compliance issues.
    A.credit risk   B.advertisement   C.market value   D.annual compliance review

99. A Wholesaler, sponsor, underwriter
    A.distributor   B.investment banker   C.ex dividend date   D.call risk

100. A Possible large gain if situation plays out as manager predicts; Depends on ability of manager to
    find special deals.
    A.special situation fund   B.investment income   C.corporate charter   D.ex dividend date

From the words provided for each clue, provide the letter of the word which best matches the clue.

101. C   A contract between an insurance company and an individual, generally guaranteeing lifetime income to the individual.
A.credit risk   B.agency basis   C.annuity   D.common stock

102. D   Auctioneer of the stock, sets the opening bid, facilitates the trade between brokers and dealers, and makes sure the best bid for the stock is executed and sold.
A.c shares   B.premium   C.contractual plan   D.specialist

103. B   Any institution or an individual meeting minimum net worth requirements for the purchase of securities qualifying under the Regulation D registration exemption.
A.equity income fund   B.accredited investor   C.bid price   D.interest rate risk

104. B   Equity Category; Portfolio: common stock in same proportions as selected index.
A.brokerage fee   B.index fund   C.constant dollars   D.conduit theory

105. C   The price at which the dealer is willing to sell the stock to an investor or another dealer.
A.total return objective   B.investment income   C.ask price   D.long

106. D   Default risk
A.american depository receipt   B.timing risk   C.annual compliance review   D.credit risk

107. B   Tax- deductible
A.bid   B.pre-tax   C.dealer   D.ask

108. D   Preferred stock that may be converted into common stock at the option of the holder.
A.timing risk   B.annual compliance review   C.all or none   D.convertible preferred stock

109. C   Date where the BOD checks if a shareholder is listed with the company, so they can get paid their dividends.
A.call option   B.international fund   C.record date   D.exchange market

110. B   Form of debt backed by stocks and or bonds of another corporation. The collateral is held by a trustee for safekeeping.
A.ex dividend date   B.collateral trust bond   C.annuity unit   D.all or none

111. B   Selection risk, business risk
A.outstanding shares   B.non-systematic risk   C.conduit theory   D.contractual plan company

112. A   To change an annuity contract from the accumulation (pay-in) stage to the distribution (payout) stage.
A.annuitize   B.insider   C.equity income fund   D.mutual fund family

113. B   The price a Market Maker will pay for a security; it's the price an investor would receive if he or she sold the security.
A.c shares   B.bid   C.agency debt   D.currency risk

114. A   Red Herring
A.preliminary prospectus   B.insider   C.dealer   D.property tax

115. A   Buy, bought, hold, or own
A.long   B.asset   C.annuity unit   D.call price

116. D   Possible loss of value due to a broad market decline. For equities, this risk is measured by a statistic called beta.
A.index fund   B.payment date   C.liquidity objective   D.market risk

117. C   A bond that may be exchanged for some other security of the issuer at the option of the holder. It is usually converted into common stock based upon a fixed conversion ratio.
A.exchange market B.contractual plan C.convertible bond D.agency debt

118. A   The price of a mutual fund. Calculates to company's funds minus liabilities divided by outstanding shares.
A.net asset value B.firm commitment C.market risk D.convertible preferred stock

119. B   Ad Valorem tax
A.cumulative voting B.property tax C.collateral trust bond D.conduit theory

120. D   Often called "Indirect Debt."
A.equity income fund B.market risk C.ask price D.agency debt

121. C   Dividend paying equities; safe, consistent income with secondary objective of growth; less volatile than other equity funds.
A.income objective B.equity income fund C.equity income fund D.timing risk

122. C   Control person, affiliate
A.annuitize B.non-systematic risk C.insider D.tax reduction objective

123. C   Growth and income fund
A.constant dollars B.american depository receipt C.equity income fund D.prepayment risk

124. D   A type of best efforts underwriting where the entire amount must be sold or the deal is called off.
A.exchange market B.tax reduction objective C.current dollars D.all or none

125. D   An accounting measure used to determine the amount of each payment during an annuity's distribution stage.
A.auction market B.current yield C.assumed interest rate D.annuity unit

126. B   The price paid for callable preferred stock or bonds redeemed by the issuer prior to maturity of the issue because interest rates have fallen.
A.aggressive growth fund B.call price C.current yield D.us goverment fund

127. B   Actual dollar amounts. Not adjusted for inflation.
A.exchange market B.current dollars C.exchange D.best efforts

128. C   Possible large gain if situation plays out as manager predicts; Depends on ability of manager to find special deals.
A.convertible bond B.call option C.special situation fund D.c shares

129. A   Dollars adjusted to show the same purchasing power from one period to another. They are "indexed" for inflation.
A.constant dollars B.blue chip stock C.bid D.outstanding shares

130. C   Contingent deferred sales charge (CDSC)
A.credit risk B.amt C.back end sales charge D.business day

131. D   Payment of a debt (principal) over a period of time in periodic installments.
A.common stock B.annuitize C.municipal bonds D.amortization

132. C   The date the security trades without its dividends. In order to get a dividend the security needs to be purchased two days prior to the record date or before the ex-dividend date.
A.timing risk B.american depository receipt C.ex dividend date D.liquidity objective

133. D   American Depository Shares
A.long B.keogh plan C.contractual plan company D.american depository receipt

134. C Has the right to receive skipped or missed dividends.
    A.balanced fund B.business day C.cumulative preferred D.aggressive growth fund

135. D Portfolio characterized by high turnover of holdings, attempts to cash in on higher-risk rapid capital appreciation situations.
    A.market risk B.annuity C.record date D.aggressive growth portfolio

136. C Alternative Minimum Tax. The requirement to add the income from tax preference items to income above an indexed level. A method to insure that wealthy persons and corporations pay at least some tax.
    A.bid B.corporate high yield fund C.amt D.accumulation stage

137. C The date the company mails out the dividend.
    A.preliminary prospectus B.timing risk C.payment date D.equity income fund

138. D Sales Charge, Sales Load
    A.bid price B.exchange C.corporate high yield fund D.brokerage fee

139. D Present yield the buyer would receive when purchasing the bond. Calculated by dividing Annual Interest rates to Market Price.
    A.outstanding shares B.preliminary prospectus C.accumulation unit D.current yield

140. B An agency Transaction
    A.duration B.agency basis C.asset D.convertible bond

141. A Cost basis
    A.contribution B.special situation fund C.distributor D.keogh plan

142. C Also called period payment plans.
    A.currency risk B.outstanding shares C.contractual plan D.total return objective

143. B Possibility that increase in general level of interest rates will drive down prices of existing fixed-income investments.
    A.amt B.interest rate risk C.appreciation D.liquidity objective

144. C Registered Representative
    A.conduit theory B.total return objective C.account executive D.timing risk

145. D The period during which contributions are made to an annuity account.
    A.annuitize B.firm commitment C.duration D.accumulation stage

146. D The price at which a dealer is willing to buy stock from an individual or another dealer.
    A.call option B.record date C.auction market D.bid price

147. A Allows the firm working for the issuing company to sell its shares the best way they can and are not responsible if shares are not sold.
    A.best efforts B.c shares C.interest rate risk D.constant dollars

148. B Mix of equities and bonds; growth with opportunity for income; portfolio mix usually under tighter constraints than growth & income fund.
    A.record date B.balanced fund C.bid D.total return objective

149. D Investment objective for investors that are willing and able to take considerable risks for the chance to hit a big financial home run.
    A.authorized stock B.appreciation C.cumulative preferred D.speculation objective

150. A   Investment objective for high-bracket investors facing a big tax bite on taxable investments may find tax-exempt vehicles produce a better after tax return.
A.tax reduction objective   B.current yield   C.exchange   D.aggressive growth portfolio

151. D   Investment objective for a combination of growth of capital and income, but less of each than investments that focus on just one of those objectives.
A.common stock   B.convertible bond   C.liquidity objective   D.total return objective

152. C   Excessive trading in a customer's account. The registered representative ignores the objectives and interest of clients and seeks only to increase commissions.
A.tax reduction objective   B.payment date   C.churning   D.debenture

153. C   Common stocks from outside of the U.S.; Exposure to exchange rate risk and political (legistlative) risk, in addition to market risk.
A.account executive   B.market risk   C.international fund   D.total return objective

154. C   Cash equivalents such as T-bills, CDs, commercial paper, BAs; Preservation of Capital; attempts to maintain $1 NAV ; used to park funds while making investment decisions.
A.b shares   B.asset   C.money market fund   D.corporate high yield fund

155. D   Tax-free bonds
A.collateral trust bond   B.convertible bond   C.outstanding shares   D.municipal bonds

156. D   unsecured Bond backed only by the good faith of the corporation. Repayment of the debt is based on the company's promise to repay.
A.income objective   B.contractual plan   C.cumulative preferred   D.debenture

157. C   Fixed-Income Securities: Possibility that homeowners will prepay mortgages more quickly than expected when interest rates fall.
A.call option   B.specialist   C.prepayment risk   D.business day

158. C   Any material designed for use by newspapers, magazines, radio, television, telephone, recordings or any other public medium to solicit business.
A.tax reduction objective   B.best efforts   C.advertisement   D.prepayment risk

159. D   Calculation of a bonds total return if held until the end of its life (maturity).
A.agency debt   B.cumulative preferred   C.contractual plan   D.yield to maturity

160. B   Switch
A.cumulative voting   B.exchange   C.firm commitment   D.conduit theory

161. B   An option to buy a specified number of shares of stock at a definite price within a specified period of time. See put option.
A.payment date   B.call option   C.bankers acceptance   D.contractual plan company

162. C   An accounting measure used to determine an annuitant's proportionate interest in the insurer's separate account during an annuity's accumulation (deposit) stage.
A.duration   B.cumulative preferred   C.accumulation unit   D.collateral trust bond

163. D   Auction market
A.accumulation unit   B.prepayment risk   C.amortization   D.exchange market

164. D   Essentially a letter of credit from a bank guaranteeing payment of a debt.
A.collateral trust bond   B.keogh plan   C.annuity unit   D.bankers acceptance

165. B   A day the New York Stock Exchange is open for business (trading).
A.ask price   B.business day   C.interest rate risk   D.yield to maturity

166. D   Small cap stocks; maximum capital appreciation; may employ short-term trading strategies; very volatile.
A.b shares   B.aggressive growth portfolio   C.contribution   D.aggressive growth fund

167. D   Bonds that cost more than the face value.
A.american depository receipt   B.annuity   C.assumed interest rate   D.premium

168. A   A stock exchange where the securities are sold to the highest bidder.
A.auction market   B.asset   C.blue chip stock   D.american depository receipt

169. A   An indication of willingness by a trader or dealer to sell a security or a commodity.
A.ask   B.exchange   C.speculation objective   D.american depository receipt

170. D   Corporate bonds rate BB
A.preliminary prospectus   B.market risk   C.net asset value   D.corporate high yield fund

171. D   Changes in value of a currency versus another currency. Current owners of forign securities may see a negative impact if foreign currency weakens against their home currency.
A.debenture   B.amt   C.advertisement   D.currency risk

172. D   The yield of the security when bought or sold prior to maturity in the secondary market. Current yield relates current income to the security's current price.
A.cumulative preferred   B.accredited investor   C.exchange market   D.current yield

173. C   Shares held by the public
A.b shares   B.current yield   C.outstanding shares   D.money market fund

174. A   Any promotional material designed for use by newspapers, magazines, billboards, radio, television, telephone recordings or other public media.
A.advertisement   B.cumulative voting   C.yield to maturity   D.interest rate risk

175. D   The increase in an asset's value.
A.duration   B.distributor   C.current yield   D.appreciation

176. C   A unit investment trust with which an investor may contact to buy mutual fund shares at fixed intervals over a fixed period of time.
A.annual compliance review   B.preliminary prospectus   C.contractual plan company   D.equity income fund

177. C   A type of shareholder voting in which the number of shares held is multiplied by the number of directors to be elected to determine the number of votes a shareholder may cast.
A.equity income fund   B.constant dollars   C.cumulative voting   D.convertible preferred stock

178. C   Anything that an individual or a corporation owns.
A.keogh plan   B.contribution   C.asset   D.account executive

179. D   The basic stock issued by a corporation representing shares of ownership.
A.yield to maturity   B.payment date   C.firm commitment   D.common stock

180. C   T-bonds, T-notes, T-bills; Income with no credit risk; may be subject to interest rate risk; the longer average maturity of the portfolio the greater the interest rate risk
A.cumulative voting   B.appreciation   C.us goverment fund   D.amortization

181. A   Bank buys issuing companies shares and sells them on the market for commission. Shares are not owned by the banks.
A.firm commitment   B.long   C.account executive   D.total return objective

182. C   Family of funds, mutual fund complex
         A.payment date   B.advertisement   C.mutual fund family   D.accumulation stage

183. C   Level Load
         A.firm commitment   B.ask   C.c shares   D.annuity unit

184. D   interest & dividends
         A.b shares   B.mutual fund family   C.accredited investor   D.investment income

185. A   The number of shares of stock that a corporation may issue.
         A.authorized stock   B.specialist   C.income objective   D.payment date

186. D   States that the issuing company wants ALL (or nothing) the shares to be sold if not, the
         underwriting is cancelled.
         A.annuity unit   B.all or none   C.common stock   D.all or none

187. B   A form of business organization in which the total worth of the organization is divided into shares of
         stock.
         A.contribution   B.corporation   C.bid price   D.collateral trust bond

188. C   A theory behind Subchapter M under which distributions to shareholders are not taxed to the
         investment company.
         A.liquidity objective   B.credit risk   C.conduit theory   D.advertisement

189. B   One who deals in securities as a principal, buying and selling for his own account.
         A.assumed interest rate   B.dealer   C.exchange market   D.amortization

190. B   Investment objective for regular production of cash from investments, through dividend or interest
         payments. Bonds and preferred stocks are often used to produce income.
         A.current dollars   B.income objective   C.insider   D.contractual plan company

191. A   The annual meeting that all registered representatives and principals must attend, the purpose of
         which is to review compliance issues.
         A.annual compliance review   B.keogh plan   C.equity income fund   D.business day

192. C   Wholesaler, sponsor, underwriter
         A.account executive   B.american depository receipt   C.distributor   D.money market fund

193. B   An HR-10 retirement Plan
         A.money market fund   B.keogh plan   C.debenture   D.preliminary prospectus

194. B   The annuity contract holder.
         A.cumulative preferred   B.annuitant   C.premium   D.call price

195. D   A base for illustrating payments from a variable annuity.
         A.current yield   B.current dollars   C.equity income fund   D.assumed interest rate

196. A   The stock of normally strong, well-established companies that have demonstrated their ability to
         pay dividends in good times and bad times.
         A.blue chip stock   B.money market fund   C.annuitize   D.prepayment risk

197. A   Investing in a specific security at an inopportune time. Dollar cost averaging is used to avoid this
         risk.
         A.timing risk   B.advertisement   C.income objective   D.us goverment fund

198. A   This is a primary need for those who never know when they will need cash quickly.
         A.liquidity objective   B.auction market   C.keogh plan   D.constant dollars

199. C Measure of the bond price in relations to the time the bond end. Taking in consideration the interest-rates, time to maturity, and differences between the coupon rate and the yield to maturity.
A.brokerage fee   B.special situation fund   C.duration   D.balanced fund

200. B Bank End Load
A.bankers acceptance   B.b shares   C.money market fund   D.credit risk

Matching

Provide the word that best matches each clue.

1. _____ Often called "Indirect Debt."

2. _____ General term for possible loss of money invested. This risk is present in most securities.

3. _____ The price of a mutual fund. Calculates to company's funds minus liabilities divided by outstanding shares.

4. _____ An accounting measure used to determine an annuitant's proportionate interest in the insurer's separate account during an annuity's accumulation (deposit) stage.

5. _____ Provides a method of handling securities-related disputes or clearing controversies between members, public customers, clearing corporations or clearing banks.

6. _____ Bank End Load

7. _____ Investment objective for regular production of cash from investments, through dividend or interest payments. Bonds and preferred stocks are often used to produce income.

8. _____ A document accompanying or part of a stock certificate that is signed by the person named on the certificate for the purpose of transferring the certificate's title to another person's name.

9. _____ Common stocks from outside of the U.S.; Exposure to exchange rate risk and political (legistlative) risk, in addition to market risk.

10. _____ The accounting measure used to determine the amount of each payment to an annuitant during the pay-out period.

11. _____ Authorized stock is the maximum number of shares a corporation may issue under the terms of its charter.

12. _____ A transaction in which a broker or dealer acts for the accounts of others by buying or selling securities on behalf of customers.

13. _____ A bond's average price is calculated by adding its face value to the price paid for it and dividing the result by two.

14. _____ American Depository Shares

15. _____ A market in which prices of securities are falling or are expected to fall.

16. _____ The stock of normally strong, well-established companies that have demonstrated their ability to pay dividends in good times and bad times.

17. _____ Corporate bonds rate BB

18. _____ Person who receives an annuity contract's distribution.

19. _____ Nominal Yield

20. _____ Ad Valorem tax

A. Agency Debt
D. Authorized Stock
G. Capital Risk
J. B shares
M. Bear Market
P. Corporate High Yield Fund
S. Coupon Rate

B. Agency Transaction
E. Annuity Unit
H. Average Price
K. Assignment
N. Accumulation Unit
Q. Net Asset Value
T. Property tax

C. American Depository Receipt
F. International Fund
I. Annuitant
L. Income Objective
O. Blue Chip Stock
R. Code of Arbitrations

Provide the word that best matches each clue.

21. _____ Income that is free from federal, and possibly state income tax; higher the investor's tax bracket, the more beneficial the tax exemption; may have some default risk; interest rate risk.

22. _____ Refers to Corporate stocks

23. _____ Date where the BOD checks if a shareholder is listed with the company, so they can get paid their dividends.

24. _____ The date the company mails out the dividend.

25. _____ Introduces new securities to the market, that advises the issuing company of the price the security will be sold for to the public.

26. _____ Educational IRA

27. _____ A theory behind Subchapter M under which distributions to shareholders are not taxed to the investment company.

28. _____ Bank End Load

29. _____ Form of debt backed by stocks and or bonds of another corporation. The collateral is held by a trustee for safekeeping.

30. _____ An HR-10 retirement Plan

31. _____ A contract between an insurance company and an individual. An annuity generally guarantees lifetime income to the person on whose life the contract is based.

32. _____ Where new issues of stock are issued. The only time when issuing companies make a profit on their shares.

33. _____ An accounting measure used to determine an annuitant's proportionate interest in the insurer's separate account during an annuity's accumulation (deposit) stage.

34. _____ Uncovered

35. _____ Buys stocks for its clients and for personal needs based on their listing price on the floor.

36. _____ Investment objective for investors that are willing and able to take considerable risks for the chance to hit a big financial home run.

37. _____ A person authorized by a court of law to liquidate an intestate decedent's estate.

38. _____ The annuity contract holder.

39. _____ Yield stated on the bonds coupon.

40. _____ Own, Hold, Purchase, Long

A. Primary Market
D. Nominal yield
G. Collateral Trust Bond
J. Annuitant
M. Speculation Objective
P. Municipal Bond Fund
S. B shares

B. Naked
E. Regular way Settlement Date
H. Annuity
K. Keogh Plan
N. Investment Banker
Q. Floor Broker
T. Payment date

C. Buy
F. Accumulation Unit
I. Conduit Theory
L. Record Date
O. Administrator
R. Coverdell

Provide the word that best matches each clue.

41. _____   A mutual fund that splits its investment assets among stocks, bonds, and other vehicles in an attempt to provide a consistent return for the investor.

42. _____   Mix of equities and bonds; growth with opportunity for income; portfolio mix usually under tighter constraints than growth & income fund.

43. _____   Any material designed for use by newspapers, magazines, radio, television, telephone, recordings or any other public medium to solicit business.

44. _____   Principal

45. _____   A stock exchange where the securities are sold to the highest bidder.

46. _____   The yield of the security when bought or sold prior to maturity in the secondary market. Current yield relates current income to the security's current price.

47. _____   Default risk

48. _____   The date the company mails out the dividend.

49. _____   A creditor

50. _____   Control person, affiliate

51. _____   Any promotional material designed for use by newspapers, magazines, billboards, radio, television, telephone recordings or other public media.

52. _____   The date on which the company declares an upcoming dividend.

53. _____   Changes in laws or rules may have negative impact on investments. The common wisdom is that political risk is high anytime Congress is in session.

54. _____   An agency Transaction

55. _____   Own, Hold, Purchase, Long

56. _____   Adjusted Gross Income. Earned income plus net passive income, portfolio income, and capital gains.

57. _____   A debt security issued by an authorized agency of the federal government.

58. _____   Possibility that principal or interest will not be paid.

59. _____ To change an annuity contract from the accumulation (pay-in) stage to the distribution (payout) stage.

60. _____ Bank End Load

A. Current Yield
D. Balanced Fund
G. Agency Basis
J. Bondholder
M. Advertisement
P. Credit risk
S. Declaration Date

B. Payment date
E. Agency Issue
H. Political Risk
K. Advertisement
N. Dealer
Q. Credit Risk
T. AGI

C. Auction Market
F. Insider
I. Annuitize
L. B shares
O. Buy
R. Asset Allocation Fund

Provide the word that best matches each clue.

61. _____ Has the right to receive skipped or missed dividends.

62. _____ Mix of equities and bonds; growth with opportunity for income; portfolio mix usually under tighter constraints than growth & income fund.

63. _____ A day the New York Stock Exchange is open for business (trading).

64. _____ Graduated tax, income tax

65. _____ Authorized stock is the maximum number of shares a corporation may issue under the terms of its charter.

66. _____ A corporate money market instrument which consists of signed promissory notes issued by the corporation to raise short-term funds.

67. _____ The Investment Company Act of 1940 requires the fund's assets be held by an independent custodian.

68. _____ A type of mutual fund that at all times some portion of its investment assets in bonds and stocks, creating a balance between the two types of securities.

69. _____ Bonds are more likely to be called when rates have dropped, forcing reinvestment of principal at lower rates.

70. _____ The increase in value of an asset. Sometimes called growth.

71. _____ Possible large gain if situation plays out as manager predicts; Depends on ability of manager to find special deals.

72. _____ The sale of investment company shares in amounts just below the point at which the sales charge is reduced on quantity.

73. _____ Coupon, coupon rate, interest

74. _____ Investing in a specific security at an inopportune time. Dollar cost averaging is used to avoid this risk.

75. _____ Level Load

76. _____ Bank buys issuing companies shares and sells them on the market for commission. Shares are not owned by the banks.

77. _____ Money on which taxes have been paid. A return of cost basis is a return of capital and not subject to tax.

78. _____ Adjusted Gross Income. Earned income plus net passive income, portfolio income, and capital gains.

79. _____ A unit investment trust with which an investor may contact to buy mutual fund shares at fixed intervals over a fixed period of time.

80. _____ An accounting measure used to determine the amount of each payment during an annuity's distribution stage.

A. Cumulative Preferred
D. Cost Basis
G. Balanced Fund
J. Balanced Fund
M. Contractual Plan Company
P. Commercial Paper
S. Firm Commitment

B. C shares
E. Custodian
H. Special Situation Fund
K. Annuity Unit
N. AGI
Q. Progressive tax
T. Appreciation

C. Breakpoint Sale
F. Nominal yield
I. Timing Risk
L. Business Day
O. Call Risk
R. Authorized Stock

Provide the word that best matches each clue.

81. _____ Has the right to receive skipped or missed dividends.

82. _____ Buy, bought, hold, or own

83. _____ Form of debt backed by stocks and or bonds of another corporation. The collateral is held by a trustee for safekeeping.

84. _____ T-bonds, T-notes, T-bills; Income with no credit risk; may be subject to interest rate risk; the longer average maturity of the portfolio the greater the interest rate risk

85. _____ Graduated tax, income tax

86. _____ A market in which prices of securities are falling or are expected to fall.

87. _____ A theory behind Subchapter M under which distributions to shareholders are not taxed to the investment company.

88. _____ Bank End Load

89. _____ Loss of income or appreciation because an investment was NOT made.

90. _____ Contingent deferred sales charge (CDSC)

91. _____ Preferred stock that may be converted into common stock at the option of the holder.

92. _____ One who deals in securities as a principal, buying and selling for his own account.

93. _____ A method of portfolio allocation and management aimed at achieving maximum return.

94. _____ An option available to mutual fund shareholders whereby fund dividends and capital gains distributions are automatically reinvested back into the fund.

95. _____ Provides a method of handling securities-related disputes or clearing controversies between members, public customers, clearing corporations or clearing banks.

96. _____ A contract between an insurance company and an individual. An annuity generally guarantees lifetime income to the person on whose life the contract is based.

97. _____ Includes an investment adviser, officer, director, partner or employee of another person.

98. _____ Common stocks from outside of the U.S.; Exposure to exchange rate risk and political (legistlative) risk, in addition to market risk.

99. _____ "New" stock

100. _____ Dollars adjusted to show the same purchasing power from one period to another. They are "indexed" for inflation.

A. International Fund
C. Aggressive Investment Agency
E. Code of Arbitrations
G. US Goverment Fund
I. B shares
K. Collateral Trust Bond
M. Long
O. Cumulative Preferred
Q. Affiliated Person
S. Annuity

B. Opportunity Cost Risk
D. Conduit Theory
F. Dealer
H. Bear Market
J. Authorized stock
L. Progressive tax
N. Back end sales charge
P. Automatic Reinvestment
R. Convertible Preferred Stock
T. Constant dollars

Provide the word that best matches each clue.

101. _____ Form of debt backed by stocks and or bonds of another corporation. The collateral is held by a trustee for safekeeping.

102. _____ Essentially a letter of credit from a bank guaranteeing payment of a debt.

103. _____ The technique of buying and selling the same financial instrument in two different markets simultaneously to take advantage of a momentary price disparity.

104. _____ Anything that an individual or a corporation owns.

105. _____ Allows the Underwriting firm to purchase any shares that the issuing company's shareholders have not bought and sell the shares themselves for a profit.

106. _____ The yield of the security when bought or sold prior to maturity in the secondary market. Current yield relates current income to the security's current price.

107. _____ A contract between an insurance company and an individual. An annuity generally guarantees lifetime income to the person on whose life the contract is based.

108. _____ Sales Charge, Sales Load

109. _____ Educational IRA

110. _____ One who deals in securities as a principal, buying and selling for his own account.

111. _____ Default risk

112. _____ A person authorized by a court of law to liquidate an intestate decedent's estate.

113. _____ Buys stocks for its clients and for personal needs based on their listing price on the floor.

114. _____ Contingent deferred sales charge (CDSC)

115. _____ The increase in an asset's value.

116. _____ Date transaction is completed and the seller pays buyer and the buyer receives the shares.

117. _____ Tax- deductible

118. _____ Current bid and asking price of security.

119. _____ Common stock from particular industry.

120. _____ Control person, affiliate

A. Floor Broker   B. Bankers Acceptance   C. Market Value
D. Sector Fund   E. Current Yield   F. Administrator
G. Settlement date   H. Annuity   I. Insider
J. Pre-tax   K. Coverdell   L. Arbitrage
M. Back end sales charge N. Standby   O. Appreciation
P. Credit risk   Q. Dealer   R. Asset
S. Collateral Trust Bond T. Brokerage fee

Provide the word that best matches each clue.

121. _____ This is the price an investor would pay when buying the security.

122. _____ Investment objective for a combination of growth of capital and income, but less of each than investments that focus on just one of those objectives.

123. _____ Equity Category; Portfolio: common stock in same proportions as selected index.

124. _____ Shares held by the public

125. _____ Auction market

126. _____ Is the price difference the Market Maker is willing to buy the stock for, to the amount he

127. _____ An annuity combining the features of the fixed and variable annuities.

128. _____ The date the company mails out the dividend.

129. _____ The stock of normally strong, well-established companies that have demonstrated their ability to pay dividends in good times and bad times.

130. _____ The net rate of investment return that must be credited to a variable life insurance policy to ensure that at all times the variable death benefit equals the amount of the death benefit.

131. _____ Control person, affiliate

132. _____ Switch

133. _____ Payment of a debt (principal) over a period of time in periodic installments.

134. _____ Corporate bonds rate BB

135. _____ The basic stock issued by a corporation representing shares of ownership.

136. _____ The interest that has accumulated since the last interest payment up to, but not including, the settlement date, and that is added to a bond transaction's contract price.

137. _____ States that the issuing company wants ALL (or nothing) the shares to be sold if not, the underwriting is cancelled.

138. _____ Adjustment bond

139. _____ Buys stocks for its clients and for personal needs based on their listing price on the floor.

140. _____ A theory behind Subchapter M under which distributions to shareholders are not taxed to the investment company.

A. Conduit Theory
D. Exchange
G. All or none
J. Insider
M. Total Return Objective
P. Exchange market
S. Common Stock

B. Combined Annuity
E. Income bond
H. Corporate High Yield Fund
K. Amortization
N. Outstanding shares
Q. Payment date
T. Spread

C. Index Fund
F. Blue Chip Stock
I. Accrued Interest
L. Floor Broker
O. Asked
R. Assumed Interest Rate

Provide the word that best matches each clue.

141. _____ A debt security backed by a loan, lease or receivables against assets other than real estate and mortgage-backed securities.

142. _____ Possibility that principal or interest will not be paid.

143. _____ Tax- deductible

144. _____ Coupon, coupon rate, interest

145. _____ Any promotional material designed for use by newspapers, magazines, billboards, radio, television, telephone recordings or other public media.

146. _____ Provides a method of handling securities-related disputes or clearing controversies between members, public customers, clearing corporations or clearing banks.

147. _____ Present yield the buyer would receive when purchasing the bond. Calculated by dividing Annual Interest rates to Market Price.

148. _____ Mix of equities and bonds; growth with opportunity for income; portfolio mix usually under tighter constraints than growth & income fund.

149. _____ Shares held by the public

150. _____ Alternative Minimum Tax. The requirement to add the income from tax preference items to income above an indexed level. A method to insure that wealthy persons and corporations pay at least some tax.

151. _____ The increase in value of an asset. Sometimes called growth.

152. _____ The basic stock issued by a corporation representing shares of ownership.

153. _____ Buys stocks for its clients and for personal needs based on their listing price on the floor.

154. _____ Open end management company.

155. _____ Adjusted Gross Income. Earned income plus net passive income, portfolio income, and capital gains.

156. _____ A type of mutual fund whose investment policy is to provide stable income with a minimum of capital risks.

157. _____ American Depository Shares

158. _____ Actual dollar amounts. Not adjusted for inflation.

159. _____ Common stock from inside and outside the U.S. Capital appreciation in whatever markets look attractive to manager.

160. _____ An option to buy a specified number of shares of stock at a definite price within a specified period of time. See put option.

A. American Depository Receipt
D. Advertisement
G. Bond Fund
J. Global Fund
M. Call Option
P. Common Stock
S. Current Dollars

B. Floor Broker
E. AGI
H. Current yield
K. Pre-tax
N. Nominal yield
Q. Balanced Fund
T. Mutual Fund

C. Credit Risk
F. Code of Arbitrations
I. Asset Backed Security
L. Outstanding shares
O. AMT
R. Appreciation

Provide the word that best matches each clue.

161. _____ An agent

162. _____ Own, Hold, Purchase, Long

163. _____ A process that allows industry disputes between members, member organizations, their employees, and customers to be heard and settled by either FINRA or a designated arbitration panel.

164. _____ Rise in general level of prices reduces the value of fixed returns.

165. _____ Measure of the bond price in relations to the time the bond end. Taking in consideration the interest-rates, time to maturity, and differences between the coupon rate and the yield to maturity.

166. _____ Alternative Minimum Tax. The requirement to add the income from tax preference items to income above an indexed level. A method to insure that wealthy persons and corporations pay at least some tax.

167. _____ Articles of Incorporation

168. _____ Tax- deductible

169. _____ Changes in laws or rules may have negative impact on investments. The common wisdom is that political risk is high anytime Congress is in session.

170. _____ Issued by most commercial banks, representing bank borrowing for a short period of time.

171. _____ The long-term gain on an asset hold for a period of longer than 12 months.

172. _____ Money on which taxes have been paid. A return of cost basis is a return of capital and not subject to tax.

173. _____ A market where sellers bid for stock and buyers sell their stock.

174. _____ Investment objective for a combination of growth of capital and income, but less of each than investments that focus on just one of those objectives.

175. _____ A base for illustrating payments from a variable annuity.

176. _____ The price at which the dealer is willing to sell the stock to an investor or another dealer.

177. _____ A type of shareholder voting in which the number of shares held is multiplied by the number of directors to be elected to determine the number of votes a shareholder may cast.

178. _____ Switch

179. _____ This is the price an investor would pay when buying the security.

180. _____ Graduated tax, income tax

A. Certification of Deposit
B. Arbitration
C. Inflationary Risk
D. Duration
E. Political Risk
F. Auction markets
G. Exchange
H. Buy
I. Ask Price
J. Progressive tax
K. Cost Basis
L. Total Return Objective
M. Pre-tax
N. Broker
O. Cumulative Voting
P. Asked
Q. Corporate Charter
R. Assumed Interest Rate
S. Capital Gain
T. AMT

Provide the word that best matches each clue.

181. _____ Cash equivalents such as T-bills, CDs, commercial paper, BAs; Preservation of Capital; attempts to maintain $1 NAV ; used to park funds while making investment decisions.

182. _____ Ability to quickly sell an investment at or near current market price. Regardless of type, more heavily traded securities are more liquid.

183. _____ A base for illustrating payments from a variable annuity.

184. _____ Mix of equities and bonds.

185. _____ Form of debt backed by stocks and or bonds of another corporation. The collateral is held by a trustee for safekeeping.

186. _____ The net rate of investment return that must be credited to a variable life insurance policy to ensure that at all times the variable death benefit equals the amount of the death benefit.

187. _____ Growth and income fund

188. _____ Graduated tax, income tax

189. _____ Shares held by the public

190. _____ Any promotional material designed for use by newspapers, magazines, billboards, radio, television, telephone recordings or other public media.

191. _____ An indication of willingness by a trader or dealer to sell a security or a commodity.

192. _____ Dollars adjusted to show the same purchasing power from one period to another. They are "indexed" for inflation.

193. _____ An annuity combining the features of the fixed and variable annuities.

194. _____ Allows the Underwriting firm to purchase any shares that the issuing company's shareholders have not bought and sell the shares themselves for a profit.

195. _____ Measure of the bond price in relations to the time the bond end. Taking in consideration the interest-rates, time to maturity, and differences between the coupon rate and the yield to maturity.

196. _____ Traditionally, the 20-day period between the filing date of a registration statement and the effective date of the registration.

197. _____ Equity Category; Portfolio: common stock in same proportions as selected index.

198. _____ The date the Board of Directors announces intention of paying dividends.

199. _____ Changes in value of a currency versus another currency. Current owners of forign securities may see a negative impact if foreign currency weakens against their home currency.

200. _____ A contract between an insurance company and an individual. An annuity generally guarantees lifetime income to the person on whose life the contract is based.

A. Equity income fund	B. Progressive tax	C. Duration
D. Cooling off Period	E. Combined Annuity	F. Standby
G. Money Market Fund	H. Ask	I. Declaration Date
J. Outstanding shares	K. Constant dollars	L. Assumed Interest Rate
M. Advertisement	N. Currency Risk	O. Annuity
P. Assumed Interest Rate	Q. Collateral Trust Bond	R. Liquidity Risk
S. Index Fund	T. Growth & Income Fund	

Provide the word that best matches each clue.

1. AGENCY DEBT   Often called "Indirect Debt."

2. CAPITAL RISK   General term for possible loss of money invested. This risk is present in most securities.

3. NET ASSET VALUE   The price of a mutual fund. Calculates to company's funds minus liabilities divided by outstanding shares.

4. ACCUMULATION UNIT   An accounting measure used to determine an annuitant's proportionate interest in the insurer's separate account during an annuity's accumulation (deposit) stage.

5. CODE OF ARBITRATIONS   Provides a method of handling securities-related disputes or clearing controversies between members, public customers, clearing corporations or clearing banks.

6. B SHARES   Bank End Load

7. INCOME OBJECTIVE   Investment objective for regular production of cash from investments, through dividend or interest payments. Bonds and preferred stocks are often used to produce income.

8. ASSIGNMENT   A document accompanying or part of a stock certificate that is signed by the person named on the certificate for the purpose of transferring the certificate's title to another person's name.

9. INTERNATIONAL FUND   Common stocks from outside of the U.S.; Exposure to exchange rate risk and political (legistlative) risk, in addition to market risk.

10. ANNUITY UNIT   The accounting measure used to determine the amount of each payment to an annuitant during the pay-out period.

11. AUTHORIZED STOCK   Authorized stock is the maximum number of shares a corporation may issue under the terms of its charter.

12. AGENCY TRANSACTION   A transaction in which a broker or dealer acts for the accounts of others by buying or selling securities on behalf of customers.

13. AVERAGE PRICE _____ A bond's average price is calculated by adding its face value to the price paid for it and dividing the result by two.

14. AMERICAN DEPOSITORY RECEIPT   American Depository Shares

15. BEAR MARKET _____ A market in which prices of securities are falling or are expected to fall.

16. BLUE CHIP STOCK _____ The stock of normally strong, well-established companies that have demonstrated their ability to pay dividends in good times and bad times.

17. CORPORATE HIGH YIELD FUND ____ Corporate bonds rate BB

18. ANNUITANT _____ Person who receives an annuity contract's distribution.

19. COUPON RATE _____ Nominal Yield

20. PROPERTY TAX _____ Ad Valorem tax

A. Agency Debt
B. Agency Transaction
C. American Depository Receipt
D. Authorized Stock
E. Annuity Unit
F. International Fund
G. Capital Risk
H. Average Price
I. Annuitant
J. B shares
K. Assignment
L. Income Objective
M. Bear Market
N. Accumulation Unit
O. Blue Chip Stock
P. Corporate High Yield Fund
Q. Net Asset Value
R. Code of Arbitrations
S. Coupon Rate
T. Property tax

Provide the word that best matches each clue.

21. MUNICIPAL BOND FUND _____ Income that is free from federal, and possibly state income tax; higher the investor's tax bracket, the more beneficial the tax exemption; may have some default risk; interest rate risk.

22. REGULAR WAY SETTLEMENT DATE   Refers to Corporate stocks

23. RECORD DATE _____ Date where the BOD checks if a shareholder is listed with the company, so they can get paid their dividends.

24. PAYMENT DATE _____ The date the company mails out the dividend.

25. INVESTMENT BANKER _____ Introduces new securities to the market, that advises the issuing company of the price the security will be sold for to the public.

26. COVERDELL _____ Educational IRA

27. CONDUIT THEORY _____   A theory behind Subchapter M under which distributions to shareholders are not taxed to the investment company.

28. B SHARES _____   Bank End Load

29. COLLATERAL TRUST BOND _____   Form of debt backed by stocks and or bonds of another corporation. The collateral is held by a trustee for safekeeping.

30. KEOGH PLAN _____   An HR-10 retirement Plan

31. ANNUITY _____   A contract between an insurance company and an individual. An annuity generally guarantees lifetime income to the person on whose life the contract is based.

32. PRIMARY MARKET _____   Where new issues of stock are issued. The only time when issuing companies make a profit on their shares.

33. ACCUMULATION UNIT _____   An accounting measure used to determine an annuitant's proportionate interest in the insurer's separate account during an annuity's accumulation (deposit) stage.

34. NAKED _____   Uncovered

35. FLOOR BROKER _____   Buys stocks for its clients and for personal needs based on their listing price on the floor.

36. SPECULATION OBJECTIVE _____   Investment objective for investors that are willing and able to take considerable risks for the chance to hit a big financial home run.

37. ADMINISTRATOR _____   A person authorized by a court of law to liquidate an intestate decedent's estate.

38. ANNUITANT _____   The annuity contract holder.

39. NOMINAL YIELD _____   Yield stated on the bonds coupon.

40. BUY _____   Own, Hold, Purchase, Long

A. Primary Market
B. Naked
C. Buy
D. Nominal yield
E. Regular way Settlement Date
F. Accumulation Unit
G. Collateral Trust Bond
H. Annuity
I. Conduit Theory
J. Annuitant
K. Keogh Plan
L. Record Date
M. Speculation Objective
N. Investment Banker
O. Administrator
P. Municipal Bond Fund
Q. Floor Broker
R. Coverdell
S. B shares
T. Payment date

Provide the word that best matches each clue.

41. ASSET ALLOCATION FUND — A mutual fund that splits its investment assets among stocks, bonds, and other vehicles in an attempt to provide a consistent return for the investor.

42. BALANCED FUND — Mix of equities and bonds; growth with opportunity for income; portfolio mix usually under tighter constraints than growth & income fund.

43. ADVERTISEMENT — Any material designed for use by newspapers, magazines, radio, television, telephone, recordings or any other public medium to solicit business.

44. DEALER — Principal

45. AUCTION MARKET — A stock exchange where the securities are sold to the highest bidder.

46. CURRENT YIELD — The yield of the security when bought or sold prior to maturity in the secondary market. Current yield relates current income to the security's current price.

47. CREDIT RISK — Default risk

48. PAYMENT DATE — The date the company mails out the dividend.

49. BONDHOLDER — A creditor

50. INSIDER — Control person, affiliate

51. ADVERTISEMENT — Any promotional material designed for use by newspapers, magazines, billboards, radio, television, telephone recordings or other public media.

52. DECLARATION DATE — The date on which the company declares an upcoming dividend.

53. POLITICAL RISK — Changes in laws or rules may have negative impact on investments. The common wisdom is that political risk is high anytime Congress is in session.

54. AGENCY BASIS — An agency Transaction

55. BUY — Own, Hold, Purchase, Long

56. AGI — Adjusted Gross Income. Earned income plus net passive income, portfolio income, and capital gains.

57. AGENCY ISSUE — A debt security issued by an authorized agency of the federal government.

58. CREDIT RISK — Possibility that principal or interest will not be paid.

59. ANNUITIZE   To change an annuity contract from the accumulation (pay-in) stage to the distribution (payout) stage.

60. B SHARES   Bank End Load

A. Current Yield
D. Balanced Fund
G. Agency Basis
J. Bondholder
M. Advertisement
P. Credit risk
S. Declaration Date

B. Payment date
E. Agency Issue
H. Political Risk
K. Advertisement
N. Dealer
Q. Credit Risk
T. AGI

C. Auction Market
F. Insider
I. Annuitize
L. B shares
O. Buy
R. Asset Allocation Fund

Provide the word that best matches each clue.

61. CUMULATIVE PREFERRED   Has the right to receive skipped or missed dividends.

62. BALANCED FUND   Mix of equities and bonds; growth with opportunity for income; portfolio mix usually under tighter constraints than growth & income fund.

63. BUSINESS DAY   A day the New York Stock Exchange is open for business (trading).

64. PROGRESSIVE TAX   Graduated tax, income tax

65. AUTHORIZED STOCK   Authorized stock is the maximum number of shares a corporation may issue under the terms of its charter.

66. COMMERCIAL PAPER   A corporate money market instrument which consists of signed promissory notes issued by the corporation to raise short-term funds.

67. CUSTODIAN   The Investment Company Act of 1940 requires the fund's assets be held by an independent custodian.

68. BALANCED FUND   A type of mutual fund that at all times some portion of its investment assets in bonds and stocks, creating a balance between the two types of securities.

69. CALL RISK   Bonds are more likely to be called when rates have dropped, forcing reinvestment of principal at lower rates.

70. APPRECIATION   The increase in value of an asset. Sometimes called growth.

71. SPECIAL SITUATION FUND   Possible large gain if situation plays out as manager predicts; Depends on ability of manager to find special deals.

72. BREAKPOINT SALE	The sale of investment company shares in amounts just below the point at which the sales charge is reduced on quantity.
73. NOMINAL YIELD	Coupon, coupon rate, interest
74. TIMING RISK	Investing in a specific security at an inopportune time. Dollar cost averaging is used to avoid this risk.
75. C SHARES	Level Load
76. FIRM COMMITMENT	Bank buys issuing companies shares and sells them on the market for commission. Shares are not owned by the banks.
77. COST BASIS	Money on which taxes have been paid. A return of cost basis is a return of capital and not subject to tax.
78. AGI	Adjusted Gross Income. Earned income plus net passive income, portfolio income, and capital gains.
79. CONTRACTUAL PLAN COMPANY	A unit investment trust with which an investor may contact to buy mutual fund shares at fixed intervals over a fixed period of time.
80. ANNUITY UNIT	An accounting measure used to determine the amount of each payment during an annuity's distribution stage.

A. Cumulative Preferred
B. C shares
C. Breakpoint Sale
D. Cost Basis
E. Custodian
F. Nominal yield
G. Balanced Fund
H. Special Situation Fund
I. Timing Risk
J. Balanced Fund
K. Annuity Unit
L. Business Day
M. Contractual Plan Company
N. AGI
O. Call Risk
P. Commercial Paper
Q. Progressive tax
R. Authorized Stock
S. Firm Commitment
T. Appreciation

Provide the word that best matches each clue.

81. CUMULATIVE PREFERRED	Has the right to receive skipped or missed dividends.
82. LONG	Buy, bought, hold, or own
83. COLLATERAL TRUST BOND	Form of debt backed by stocks and or bonds of another corporation. The collateral is held by a trustee for safekeeping.

84.	US GOVERMENT FUND	T-bonds, T-notes, T-bills; Income with no credit risk; may be subject to interest rate risk; the longer average maturity of the portfolio the greater the interest rate risk
85.	PROGRESSIVE TAX	Graduated tax, income tax
86.	BEAR MARKET	A market in which prices of securities are falling or are expected to fall.
87.	CONDUIT THEORY	A theory behind Subchapter M under which distributions to shareholders are not taxed to the investment company.
88.	B SHARES	Bank End Load
89.	OPPORTUNITY COST RISK	Loss of income or appreciation because an investment was NOT made.
90.	BACK END SALES CHARGE	Contingent deferred sales charge (CDSC)
91.	CONVERTIBLE PREFERRED STOCK	Preferred stock that may be converted into common stock at the option of the holder.
92.	DEALER	One who deals in securities as a principal, buying and selling for his own account.
93.	AGGRESSIVE INVESTMENT AGENCY	A method of portfolio allocation and management aimed at achieving maximum return.
94.	AUTOMATIC REINVESTMENT	An option available to mutual fund shareholders whereby fund dividends and capital gains distributions are automatically reinvested back into the fund.
95.	CODE OF ARBITRATIONS	Provides a method of handling securities-related disputes or clearing controversies between members, public customers, clearing corporations or clearing banks.
96.	ANNUITY	A contract between an insurance company and an individual. An annuity generally guarantees lifetime income to the person on whose life the contract is based.
97.	AFFILIATED PERSON	Includes an investment adviser, officer, director, partner or employee of another person.
98.	INTERNATIONAL FUND	Common stocks from outside of the U.S.; Exposure to exchange rate risk and political (legistlative) risk, in addition to market risk.

99. AUTHORIZED STOCK   "New" stock

100. CONSTANT DOLLARS   Dollars adjusted to show the same purchasing power from one period to another. They are "indexed" for inflation.

A. International Fund	B. Opportunity Cost Risk
C. Aggressive Investment Agency	D. Conduit Theory
E. Code of Arbitrations	F. Dealer
G. US Goverment Fund	H. Bear Market
I. B shares	J. Authorized stock
K. Collateral Trust Bond	L. Progressive tax
M. Long	N. Back end sales charge
O. Cumulative Preferred	P. Automatic Reinvestment
Q. Affiliated Person	R. Convertible Preferred Stock
S. Annuity	T. Constant dollars

Provide the word that best matches each clue.

101. COLLATERAL TRUST BOND   Form of debt backed by stocks and or bonds of another corporation. The collateral is held by a trustee for safekeeping.

102. BANKERS ACCEPTANCE   Essentially a letter of credit from a bank guaranteeing payment of a debt.

103. ARBITRAGE   The technique of buying and selling the same financial instrument in two different markets simultaneously to take advantage of a momentary price disparity.

104. ASSET   Anything that an individual or a corporation owns.

105. STANDBY   Allows the Underwriting firm to purchase any shares that the issuing company's shareholders have not bought and sell the shares themselves for a profit.

106. CURRENT YIELD   The yield of the security when bought or sold prior to maturity in the secondary market. Current yield relates current income to the security's current price.

107. ANNUITY   A contract between an insurance company and an individual. An annuity generally guarantees lifetime income to the person on whose life the contract is based.

108. BROKERAGE FEE   Sales Charge, Sales Load

109. COVERDELL   Educational IRA

110. DEALER   One who deals in securities as a principal, buying and selling for his own account.

111. CREDIT RISK	Default risk	
112. ADMINISTRATOR	A person authorized by a court of law to liquidate an intestate decedent's estate.	
113. FLOOR BROKER	Buys stocks for its clients and for personal needs based on their listing price on the floor.	
114. BACK END SALES CHARGE	Contingent deferred sales charge (CDSC)	
115. APPRECIATION	The increase in an asset's value.	
116. SETTLEMENT DATE	Date transaction is completed and the seller pays buyer and the buyer receives the shares.	
117. PRE-TAX	Tax- deductible	
118. MARKET VALUE	Current bid and asking price of security.	
119. SECTOR FUND	Common stock from particular industry.	
120. INSIDER	Control person, affiliate	

A. Floor Broker
D. Sector Fund
G. Settlement date
J. Pre-tax
M. Back end sales charge
P. Credit risk
S. Collateral Trust Bond

B. Bankers Acceptance
E. Current Yield
H. Annuity
K. Coverdell
N. Standby
Q. Dealer
T. Brokerage fee

C. Market Value
F. Administrator
I. Insider
L. Arbitrage
O. Appreciation
R. Asset

Provide the word that best matches each clue.

121. ASKED	This is the price an investor would pay when buying the security.
122. TOTAL RETURN OBJECTIVE	Investment objective for a combination of growth of capital and income, but less of each than investments that focus on just one of those objectives.
123. INDEX FUND	Equity Category; Portfolio: common stock in same proportions as selected index.
124. OUTSTANDING SHARES	Shares held by the public
125. EXCHANGE MARKET	Auction market
126. SPREAD	Is the price difference the Market Maker is willing to buy the stock for, to the amount he
127. COMBINED ANNUITY	An annuity combining the features of the fixed and variable annuities.

128. PAYMENT DATE _____   The date the company mails out the dividend.

129. BLUE CHIP STOCK _____   The stock of normally strong, well-established companies that have demonstrated their ability to pay dividends in good times and bad times.

130. ASSUMED INTEREST RATE _____   The net rate of investment return that must be credited to a variable life insurance policy to ensure that at all times the variable death benefit equals the amount of the death benefit.

131. INSIDER _____   Control person, affiliate

132. EXCHANGE _____   Switch

133. AMORTIZATION _____   Payment of a debt (principal) over a period of time in periodic installments.

134. CORPORATE HIGH YIELD FUND _____   Corporate bonds rate BB

135. COMMON STOCK _____   The basic stock issued by a corporation representing shares of ownership.

136. ACCRUED INTEREST _____   The interest that has accumulated since the last interest payment up to, but not including, the settlement date, and that is added to a bond transaction's contract price.

137. ALL OR NONE _____   States that the issuing company wants ALL (or nothing) the shares to be sold if not, the underwriting is cancelled.

138. INCOME BOND _____   Adjustment bond

139. FLOOR BROKER _____   Buys stocks for its clients and for personal needs based on their listing price on the floor.

140. CONDUIT THEORY _____   A theory behind Subchapter M under which distributions to shareholders are not taxed to the investment company.

A. Conduit Theory
D. Exchange
G. All or none
J. Insider
M. Total Return Objective
P. Exchange market
S. Common Stock

B. Combined Annuity
E. Income bond
H. Corporate High Yield Fund
K. Amortization
N. Outstanding shares
Q. Payment date
T. Spread

C. Index Fund
F. Blue Chip Stock
I. Accrued Interest
L. Floor Broker
O. Asked
R. Assumed Interest Rate

Provide the word that best matches each clue.

141. ASSET BACKED SECURITY — A debt security backed by a loan, lease or receivables against assets other than real estate and mortgage-backed securities.

142. CREDIT RISK — Possibility that principal or interest will not be paid.

143. PRE-TAX — Tax- deductible

144. NOMINAL YIELD — Coupon, coupon rate, interest

145. ADVERTISEMENT — Any promotional material designed for use by newspapers, magazines, billboards, radio, television, telephone recordings or other public media.

146. CODE OF ARBITRATIONS — Provides a method of handling securities-related disputes or clearing controversies between members, public customers, clearing corporations or clearing banks.

147. CURRENT YIELD — Present yield the buyer would receive when purchasing the bond. Calculated by dividing Annual Interest rates to Market Price.

148. BALANCED FUND — Mix of equities and bonds; growth with opportunity for income; portfolio mix usually under tighter constraints than growth & income fund.

149. OUTSTANDING SHARES — Shares held by the public

150. AMT — Alternative Minimum Tax. The requirement to add the income from tax preference items to income above an indexed level. A method to insure that wealthy persons and corporations pay at least some tax.

151. APPRECIATION — The increase in value of an asset. Sometimes called growth.

152. COMMON STOCK — The basic stock issued by a corporation representing shares of ownership.

153. FLOOR BROKER — Buys stocks for its clients and for personal needs based on their listing price on the floor.

154. MUTUAL FUND — Open end management company.

155. AGI _____ Adjusted Gross Income. Earned income plus net passive income, portfolio income, and capital gains.

156. BOND FUND _____ A type of mutual fund whose investment policy is to provide stable income with a minimum of capital risks.

157. AMERICAN DEPOSITORY RECEIPT American Depository Shares

158. CURRENT DOLLARS _____ Actual dollar amounts. Not adjusted for inflation.

159. GLOBAL FUND _____ Common stock from inside and outside the U.S. Capital appreciation in whatever markets look attractive to manager.

160. CALL OPTION _____ An option to buy a specified number of shares of stock at a definite price within a specified period of time. See put option.

A. American Depository Receipt
B. Floor Broker
C. Credit Risk
D. Advertisement
E. AGI
F. Code of Arbitrations
G. Bond Fund
H. Current yield
I. Asset Backed Security
J. Global Fund
K. Pre-tax
L. Outstanding shares
M. Call Option
N. Nominal yield
O. AMT
P. Common Stock
Q. Balanced Fund
R. Appreciation
S. Current Dollars
T. Mutual Fund

Provide the word that best matches each clue.

161. BROKER _____ An agent

162. BUY _____ Own, Hold, Purchase, Long

163. ARBITRATION _____ A process that allows industry disputes between members, member organizations, their employees, and customers to be heard and settled by either FINRA or a designated arbitration panel.

164. INFLATIONARY RISK _____ Rise in general level of prices reduces the value of fixed returns.

165. DURATION _____ Measure of the bond price in relations to the time the bond end. Taking in consideration the interest-rates, time to maturity, and differences between the coupon rate and the yield to maturity.

166. AMT _____ Alternative Minimum Tax. The requirement to add the income from tax preference items to income above an indexed level. A method to insure that wealthy persons and corporations pay at least some tax.

167. CORPORATE CHARTER — Articles of Incorporation

168. PRE-TAX — Tax- deductible

169. POLITICAL RISK — Changes in laws or rules may have negative impact on investments. The common wisdom is that political risk is high anytime Congress is in session.

170. CERTIFICATION OF DEPOSIT — Issued by most commercial banks, representing bank borrowing for a short period of time.

171. CAPITAL GAIN — The long-term gain on an asset hold for a period of longer than 12 months.

172. COST BASIS — Money on which taxes have been paid. A return of cost basis is a return of capital and not subject to tax.

173. AUCTION MARKETS — A market where sellers bid for stock and buyers sell their stock.

174. TOTAL RETURN OBJECTIVE — Investment objective for a combination of growth of capital and income, but less of each than investments that focus on just one of those objectives.

175. ASSUMED INTEREST RATE — A base for illustrating payments from a variable annuity.

176. ASK PRICE — The price at which the dealer is willing to sell the stock to an investor or another dealer.

177. CUMULATIVE VOTING — A type of shareholder voting in which the number of shares held is multiplied by the number of directors to be elected to determine the number of votes a shareholder may cast.

178. EXCHANGE — Switch

179. ASKED — This is the price an investor would pay when buying the security.

180. PROGRESSIVE TAX — Graduated tax, income tax

A. Certification of Deposit
B. Arbitration
C. Inflationary Risk
D. Duration
E. Political Risk
F. Auction markets
G. Exchange
H. Buy
I. Ask Price
J. Progressive tax
K. Cost Basis
L. Total Return Objective
M. Pre-tax
N. Broker
O. Cumulative Voting
P. Asked
Q. Corporate Charter
R. Assumed Interest Rate
S. Capital Gain
T. AMT

Provide the word that best matches each clue.

181. MONEY MARKET FUND — Cash equivalents such as T-bills, CDs, commercial paper, BAs; Preservation of Capital; attempts to maintain $1 NAV ; used to park funds while making investment decisions.

182. LIQUIDITY RISK — Ability to quickly sell an investment at or near current market price. Regardless of type, more heavily traded securities are more liquid.

183. ASSUMED INTEREST RATE — A base for illustrating payments from a variable annuity.

184. GROWTH & INCOME FUND — Mix of equities and bonds.

185. COLLATERAL TRUST BOND — Form of debt backed by stocks and or bonds of another corporation. The collateral is held by a trustee for safekeeping.

186. ASSUMED INTEREST RATE — The net rate of investment return that must be credited to a variable life insurance policy to ensure that at all times the variable death benefit equals the amount of the death benefit.

187. EQUITY INCOME FUND — Growth and income fund

188. PROGRESSIVE TAX — Graduated tax, income tax

189. OUTSTANDING SHARES — Shares held by the public

190. ADVERTISEMENT — Any promotional material designed for use by newspapers, magazines, billboards, radio, television, telephone recordings or other public media.

191. ASK — An indication of willingness by a trader or dealer to sell a security or a commodity.

192. CONSTANT DOLLARS — Dollars adjusted to show the same purchasing power from one period to another. They are "indexed" for inflation.

193. COMBINED ANNUITY — An annuity combining the features of the fixed and variable annuities.

194. STANDBY — Allows the Underwriting firm to purchase any shares that the issuing company's shareholders have not bought and sell the shares themselves for a profit.

195. DURATION — Measure of the bond price in relations to the time the bond end. Taking in consideration the interest-rates, time to maturity, and differences between the coupon rate and the yield to maturity.

196. COOLING OFF PERIOD _____ Traditionally, the 20-day period between the filing date of a registration statement and the effective date of the registration.

197. INDEX FUND _____ Equity Category; Portfolio: common stock in same proportions as selected index.

198. DECLARATION DATE _____ The date the Board of Directors announces intention of paying dividends.

199. CURRENCY RISK _____ Changes in value of a currency versus another currency. Current owners of forign securities may see a negative impact if foreign currency weakens against their home currency.

200. ANNUITY _____ A contract between an insurance company and an individual. An annuity generally guarantees lifetime income to the person on whose life the contract is based.

A. Equity income fund
B. Progressive tax
C. Duration
D. Cooling off Period
E. Combined Annuity
F. Standby
G. Money Market Fund
H. Ask
I. Declaration Date
J. Outstanding shares
K. Constant dollars
L. Assumed Interest Rate
M. Advertisement
N. Currency Risk
O. Annuity
P. Assumed Interest Rate
Q. Collateral Trust Bond
R. Liquidity Risk
S. Index Fund
T. Growth & Income Fund

Word Search

Find the hidden words. The words have been placed horizontally, vertically, or diagonally. When you locate a word, draw a circle around it.

Q	N	U	A	S	K	P	R	I	C	E	G	X	H	L	L	O	N	G	Y
L	I	Q	U	I	D	I	T	Y	R	I	S	K	H	C	M	O	M	S	E
V	K	W	A	C	R	E	D	I	T	R	I	S	K	L	G	M	O	D	O
A	D	K	R	I	N	V	E	S	T	M	E	N	T	I	N	C	O	M	E
E	A	L	L	O	R	N	O	E	U	B	U	Y	M	G	B	D	W	W	
H	Q	H	S	S	M	A	R	K	E	T	R	I	S	K	D	I	K	V	M
R	T	I	M	I	N	G	R	I	S	K	K	C	K	Z	O	D	V	H	P
H	P	R	O	G	R	E	S	S	I	V	E	T	A	X	E	P	Y	Q	S
W	C	L	A	S	S	A	S	H	A	R	E	S	E	A	A	R	G	C	H
C	O	M	M	O	N	S	T	O	C	K	A	H	I	S	W	I	H	N	T
P	H	A	G	E	N	C	Y	B	A	S	I	S	S	K	C	C	B	T	R
W	P	A	A	A	P	P	R	E	C	I	A	T	I	O	N	E	R	Q	Y

1. interest & dividends
2. Buy, bought, hold, or own
3. Ability to quickly sell an investment at or near current market price. Regardless of type, more heavily traded securities are more liquid.
4. To offer
5. Investing in a specific security at an inopportune time. Dollar cost averaging is used to avoid this risk.
6. Possibility that principal or interest will not be paid.
7. The price at which a dealer is willing to buy stock from an individual or another dealer.
8. The basic stock issued by a corporation representing shares of ownership.
9. Systematic risk
10. The increase in value of an asset. Sometimes called growth.
11. An agency Transaction
12. The price at which the dealer is willing to sell the stock to an investor or another dealer.
13. Front end sales charge, front end load
14. Graduated tax, income tax
15. States that the issuing company wants ALL (or nothing) the shares to be sold if not, the underwriting is cancelled.
16. The accounting measure used to determine the amount of each payment to an annuitant during the pay-out period.
17. Own, Hold, Purchase, Long

A. Progressive tax
B. Liquidity Risk
C. Investment income
D. Market risk
E. Timing Risk
F. Ask
G. Bid Price
H. Ask Price
I. Buy
J. Appreciation
K. Common Stock
L. Credit Risk
M. Annuity Unit
N. Agency Basis
O. All or none
P. Class A shares
Q. Long

2. *Find the hidden words. The words have been placed horizontally, vertically, or diagonally. When you locate a word, draw a circle around it.*

M	U	T	U	A	L	F	U	N	D	F	A	M	I	L	Y	F	R	M	W
A	U	C	T	I	O	N	M	A	R	K	E	T	S	R	X	Q	Y	U	K
O	R	I	N	D	E	X	F	U	N	D	W	A	M	T	H	B	N	T	M
J	C	A	P	P	R	E	C	I	A	T	I	O	N	G	C	R	L	U	D
C	U	M	U	L	A	T	I	V	E	V	O	T	I	N	G	O	V	A	E
D	E	C	L	A	R	A	T	I	O	N	D	A	T	E	F	K	Z	L	B
C	O	O	L	I	N	G	O	F	F	P	E	R	I	O	D	E	W	F	E
C	U	R	R	E	N	T	D	O	L	L	A	R	S	E	C	R	F	U	N
Z	V	H	D	A	G	E	N	C	Y	D	E	B	T	A	P	M	I	N	T
U	Q	M	M	O	N	E	Y	M	A	R	K	E	T	F	U	N	D	D	U
E	A	C	C	R	U	E	D	I	N	T	E	R	E	S	T	K	W	V	R
F	T	L	O	N	G	A	S	P	R	E	A	D	A	V	E	R	A	G	E

1. Often called "Indirect Debt."
2. An agent
3. Alternative Minimum Tax. The requirement to add the income from tax preference items to income above an indexed level. A method to insure that wealthy persons and corporations pay at least some tax.
4. Actual dollar amounts. Not adjusted for inflation.
5. The date on which the company declares an upcoming dividend.
6. The interest that has accumulated since the last interest payment up to, but not including, the settlement date, and that is added to a bond transaction's contract price.
7. A price at a midpoint among a number of prices. Technical analysts often use averages as market indicators.
8. Family of funds, mutual fund complex
9. Traditionally, the 20-day period between the filing date of a registration statement and the effective date of the registration.
10. Equity Category; Portfolio: common stock in same proportions as selected index.
11. The increase in value of an asset. Sometimes called growth.
12. A type of shareholder voting in which the number of shares held is multiplied by the number of directors to be elected to determine the number of votes a shareholder may cast.
13. unsecured Bond backed only by the good faith of the corporation. Repayment of the debt is based on the company's promise to repay.
14. Buy, bought, hold, or own
15. Cash equivalents such as T-bills, CDs, commercial paper, BAs; Preservation of Capital; attempts to maintain $1 NAV ; used to park funds while making investment decisions.
16. Open end management company.
17. Is the price difference the Market Maker is willing to buy the stock for, to the amount he
18. Any institution or an individual meeting minimum net worth requirements for the purchase of securities qualifying under the Regulation D registration exemption.
19. A market where sellers bid for stock and buyers sell their stock.

A. Index Fund
E. AMT
I. Mutual Fund Family
M. Broker
Q. Debenture

B. Average
F. Accrued Interest
J. Auction markets
N. Appreciation
R. Accredited Investor

C. Cumulative Voting
G. Money Market Fund
K. Agency Debt
O. Declaration Date
S. Spread

D. Current Dollars
H. Long
L. Mutual Fund
P. Cooling off Period

3. *Find the hidden words. The words have been placed horizontally, vertically, or diagonally. When you locate a word, draw a circle around it.*

F	T	G	F	E	X	D	I	V	I	D	E	N	D	D	A	T	E	G	M
N	I	N	T	E	R	N	A	T	I	O	N	A	L	F	U	N	D	L	U
X	G	I	N	V	E	S	T	M	E	N	T	B	A	N	K	E	R	O	U
S	F	B	I	D	V	R	O	S	R	D	E	A	L	E	R	C	C	B	K
R	H	V	E	B	A	L	A	N	C	E	D	F	U	N	D	R	T	A	Q
C	R	E	D	I	T	R	I	S	K	B	S	O	A	A	G	V	Z	L	J
Z	C	A	P	I	T	A	L	S	T	R	U	C	T	U	R	E	T	F	J
U	N	E	T	A	S	S	E	T	V	A	L	U	E	J	C	I	R	U	P
O	A	U	T	H	O	R	I	Z	E	D	S	T	O	C	K	U	U	N	P
R	F	M	U	N	I	C	I	P	A	L	B	O	N	D	F	U	N	D	S
C	I	D	E	C	L	A	R	A	T	I	O	N	D	A	T	E	J	X	Y
B	N	B	A	C	K	E	N	D	S	A	L	E	S	C	H	A	R	G	E

1. Income that is free from federal, and possibly state income tax; higher the investor's tax bracket, the more beneficial the tax exemption; may have some default risk; interest rate risk.
2. Common stock from inside and outside the U.S. Capital appreciation in whatever markets look attractive to manager.
3. The price a Market Maker will pay for a security; it's the price an investor would receive if he or she sold the security.
4. The amount of debt or equity issued by a corporation.
5. Principal
6. Common stocks from outside of the U.S.; Exposure to exchange rate risk and political (legistlative) risk, in addition to market risk.
7. Mix of equities and bonds; growth with opportunity for income; portfolio mix usually under tighter constraints than growth & income fund.
8. "New" stock
9. The date on which the company declares an upcoming dividend.
10. Contingent deferred sales charge (CDSC)
11. Default risk
12. Introduces new securities to the market, that advises the issuing company of the price the security will be sold for to the public.
13. The price of a mutual fund. Calculates to company's funds minus liabilities divided by outstanding shares.
14. The date the security trades without its dividends. In order to get a dividend the security needs to be purchased two days prior to the record date or before the ex-dividend date.
15. A base for illustrating payments from a variable annuity.
16. The stock of normally strong, well-established companies that have demonstrated their ability to pay dividends in good times and bad times.
17. A theory behind Subchapter M under which distributions to shareholders are not taxed to the investment company.
18. Investment objective for investors that are willing and able to take considerable risks for the chance to hit a big financial home run.

A. Back end sales charge
B. Speculation Objective
C. International Fund
D. Balanced Fund
E. Blue Chip Stock
F. Capital Structure
G. Credit risk
H. Conduit Theory
I. Authorized stock
J. Ex dividend Date
K. Bid
L. Municipal Bond Fund
M. Global Fund
N. Investment Banker
O. Net Asset Value
P. Assumed Interest Rate
Q. Dealer
R. Declaration Date

4. *Find the hidden words. The words have been placed horizontally, vertically, or diagonally. When you locate a word, draw a circle around it.*

S	X	S	F	R	U	S	Z	C	U	S	T	O	D	I	A	N	Z	S	F
S	P	E	C	I	A	L	S	I	T	U	A	T	I	O	N	F	U	N	D
T	X	T	I	I	N	C	O	M	E	O	B	J	E	C	T	I	V	E	B
O	Y	D	O	C	A	C	C	R	U	E	D	I	N	T	E	R	E	S	T
Y	V	M	A	C	A	L	L	P	R	O	V	I	S	I	O	N	S	J	H
Y	X	M	C	O	S	T	B	A	S	I	S	C	K	X	F	Q	W	Q	X
R	W	X	P	G	R	O	W	T	H	O	B	J	E	C	T	I	V	E	V
B	J	A	L	L	O	R	N	O	N	E	A	N	N	U	I	T	I	Z	E
Y	C	R	E	D	I	T	R	I	S	K	E	X	C	H	A	N	G	E	H
Z	T	C	O	N	D	U	I	T	T	H	E	O	R	Y	H	U	Y	U	M
C	O	U	P	O	N	R	A	T	E	R	E	C	O	R	D	D	A	T	E
L	C	O	N	V	E	R	T	I	B	L	E	B	O	N	D	U	B	G	F

1. Investment objective for regular production of cash from investments, through dividend or interest payments. Bonds and preferred stocks are often used to produce income.
2. Possibility that principal or interest will not be paid.
3. Switch
4. A theory behind Subchapter M under which distributions to shareholders are not taxed to the investment company.
5. The Investment Company Act of 1940 requires the fund's assets be held by an independent custodian.
6. Possible large gain if situation plays out as manager predicts; Depends on ability of manager to find special deals.
7. Nominal Yield
8. A bond that may be exchanged for some other security of the issuer at the option of the holder. It is usually converted into common stock based upon a fixed conversion ratio.
9. The interest that has accumulated since the last interest payment up to, but not including, the settlement date, and that is added to a bond transaction's contract price.
10. Investment objective for increase in invested capital, primarily generated through price appreciation. Equity securities (stocks) are usually used in pursuit of this goal.
11. An issuing corporation retains the privilege of recalling (redeeming) its issues of equity or debt.
12. States that the issuing company wants ALL (or nothing) the shares to be sold if not, the underwriting is cancelled.
13. To change an annuity contract from the accumulation (pay-in) stage to the distribution (payout) stage.
14. A debt security issued by an authorized agency of the federal government.
15. Registered Representative
16. Money on which taxes have been paid. A return of cost basis is a return of capital and not subject to tax.
17. Date where the BOD checks if a shareholder is listed with the company, so they can get paid their dividends.
18. Principal Risk

A. Credit Risk
E. Income Objective
I. Account Executive
M. Convertible Bond
Q. All or none

B. Coupon Rate
F. Special Situation Fund
J. Growth Objective
N. Conduit Theory
R. Call Provisions

C. Annuitize
G. Capital Risk
K. Agency Issue
O. Accrued Interest

D. Cost Basis
H. Exchange
L. Record Date
P. Custodian

5. *Find the hidden words. The words have been placed horizontally, vertically, or diagonally. When you locate a word, draw a circle around it.*

I	N	C	O	D	E	O	F	A	R	B	I	T	R	A	T	I	O	N	S
D	E	B	E	N	T	U	R	E	S	E	C	T	O	R	F	U	N	D	T
C	B	A	C	K	E	N	D	S	A	L	E	S	C	H	A	R	G	E	S
C	A	G	E	N	C	Y	D	E	B	T	N	P	V	V	S	C	M	L	T
A	R	H	S	H	Q	C	O	N	T	R	I	B	U	T	I	O	N	N	A
L	D	U	P	S	P	E	C	I	A	L	I	S	T	C	B	C	I	F	N
L	P	R	R	E	A	N	N	U	A	L	R	E	T	U	R	N	Q	A	D
R	K	U	E	W	V	J	S	J	A	N	N	U	I	T	A	N	T	S	B
I	J	E	A	M	A	D	V	E	R	T	I	S	E	M	E	N	T	S	Y
S	H	M	D	O	D	P	A	U	C	T	I	O	N	M	A	R	K	E	T
K	W	H	W	B	R	E	A	K	P	O	I	N	T	S	A	L	E	T	C
Q	N	W	X	Q	H	A	U	C	T	I	O	N	M	A	R	K	E	T	S

1. Allows the Underwriting firm to purchase any shares that the issuing company's shareholders have not bought and sell the shares themselves for a profit.
2. Is the price difference the Market Maker is willing to buy the stock for, to the amount he
3. A market where sellers bid for stock and buyers sell their stock.
4. A stock exchange where the securities are sold to the highest bidder.
5. Anything that an individual or a corporation owns.
6. Holding period return
7. The sale of investment company shares in amounts just below the point at which the sales charge is reduced on quantity.
8. Bonds are more likely to be called when rates have dropped, forcing reinvestment of principal at lower rates.
9. Often called "Indirect Debt."
10. Any promotional material designed for use by newspapers, magazines, billboards, radio, television, telephone recordings or other public media.
11. Cost basis
12. Common stock from particular industry.
13. Provides a method of handling securities-related disputes or clearing controversies between members, public customers, clearing corporations or clearing banks.
14. Person who receives an annuity contract's distribution.
15. unsecured Bond backed only by the good faith of the corporation. Repayment of the debt is based on the company's promise to repay.
16. Auctioneer of the stock, sets the opening bid, facilitates the trade between brokers and dealers, and makes sure the best bid for the stock is executed and sold.
17. Contingent deferred sales charge (CDSC)
18. The stock of normally strong, well-established companies that have demonstrated their ability to pay dividends in good times and bad times.

A. Code of Arbitrations	B. Sector Fund	C. Advertisement	D. Asset
E. Back end sales charge	F. Auction Market	G. Spread	H. Specialist
I. Annual return	J. Breakpoint Sale	K. Auction markets	L. Call Risk
M. Standby	N. Debenture	O. Blue Chip Stock	P. Annuitant
Q. Agency Debt	R. Contribution		

6.

Find the hidden words. The words have been placed horizontally, vertically, or diagonally. When you locate a word, draw a circle around it.

E	D	G	F	A	O	M	V	M	A	R	B	I	T	R	A	T	I	O	N
L	E	K	T	G	X	G	Q	A	B	U	S	I	N	E	S	S	D	A	Y
A	G	I	I	E	B	C	U	R	R	E	N	T	Y	I	E	L	D	Z	Y
X	M	B	M	N	W	H	N	K	Y	C	R	E	D	I	T	R	I	S	K
M	L	X	I	T	T	P	N	E	C	O	X	F	O	E	O	D	D	P	Z
L	A	J	N	P	O	L	I	T	I	C	A	L	R	I	S	K	S	R	P
Q	U	C	G	S	P	J	W	V	I	N	C	O	M	E	B	O	N	D	U
Z	R	E	R	T	B	A	L	A	N	C	E	D	F	U	N	D	T	Q	T
M	U	N	I	C	I	P	A	L	B	O	N	D	S	G	Y	C	V	Z	B
C	W	A	S	K	E	D	K	U	V	T	T	R	A	D	E	D	A	T	E
W	B	K	K	A	P	P	R	E	C	I	A	T	I	O	N	H	D	F	U
W	H	Y	M	C	R	E	D	I	T	R	I	S	K	V	M	F	B	L	O

1. Current bid and asking price of security.
2. Changes in laws or rules may have negative impact on investments. The common wisdom is that political risk is high anytime Congress is in session.
3. Present yield the buyer would receive when purchasing the bond. Calculated by dividing Annual Interest rates to Market Price.
4. Tax-free bonds
5. Investing in a specific security at an inopportune time. Dollar cost averaging is used to avoid this risk.
6. Date transaction is executed.
7. Default risk
8. Mix of equities and bonds; growth with opportunity for income; portfolio mix usually under tighter constraints than growth & income fund.
9. A process that allows industry disputes between members, member organizations, their employees, and customers to be heard and settled by either FINRA or a designated arbitration panel.
10. A day the New York Stock Exchange is open for business (trading).
11. Adjusted Gross Income. Earned income plus net passive income, portfolio income, and capital gains.
12. Adjustment bond
13. An individual or a firm that effects securities transactions for the accounts of others.
14. The increase in value of an asset. Sometimes called growth.
15. Possibility that principal or interest will not be paid.
16. This is the price an investor would pay when buying the security.

A. Agent
B. Income bond
C. Political Risk
D. Current yield
E. Municipal bonds
F. Business Day
G. Balanced Fund
H. Arbitration
I. Timing Risk
J. Trade date
K. AGI
L. Credit Risk
M. Market Value
N. Credit risk
O. Asked
P. Appreciation

7. *Find the hidden words. The words have been placed horizontally, vertically, or diagonally. When you locate a word, draw a circle around it.*

N	A	S	S	E	T	A	L	L	O	C	A	T	I	O	N	F	U	N	D
K	J	K	Y	G	C	L	A	S	S	A	S	H	A	R	E	S	E	C	H
X	R	S	T	A	N	D	B	Y	N	N	X	D	E	A	L	E	R	R	
W	V	M	E	Q	U	I	T	Y	I	N	C	O	M	E	F	U	N	D	U
C	A	P	I	T	A	L	S	T	R	U	C	T	U	R	E	J	R	O	Y
Y	X	J	U	U	C	P	N	O	M	I	N	A	L	Y	I	E	L	D	Q
Y	Q	A	C	C	U	M	U	L	A	T	I	O	N	U	N	I	T	N	J
A	S	S	I	G	N	M	E	N	T	A	A	L	J	Y	V	F	F	V	I
C	I	T	B	U	Y	R	S	A	N	N	U	A	L	R	E	T	U	R	N
H	B	X	Y	L	A	D	V	E	R	T	I	S	E	M	E	N	T	L	M
P	M	K	A	U	T	H	O	R	I	Z	E	D	S	T	O	C	K	Z	S
G	T	X	C	U	R	R	E	N	T	Y	I	E	L	D	A	N	R	L	M

1. Present yield the buyer would receive when purchasing the bond. Calculated by dividing Annual Interest rates to Market Price.
2. The annuity contract holder.
3. A mutual fund that splits its investment assets among stocks, bonds, and other vehicles in an attempt to provide a consistent return for the investor.
4. Authorized stock is the maximum number of shares a corporation may issue under the terms of its charter.
5. The amount of debt or equity issued by a corporation.
6. Growth and income fund
7. Possible large gain if situation plays out as manager predicts; Depends on ability of manager to find special deals.
8. Front end sales charge, front end load
9. Principal
10. Holding period return
11. The number of shares of stock that a corporation may issue.
12. Coupon, coupon rate, interest
13. Buys stocks for its clients and for personal needs based on their listing price on the floor.
14. An accounting measure used to determine an annuitant's proportionate interest in the insurer's separate account during an annuity's accumulation (deposit) stage.
15. Any promotional material designed for use by newspapers, magazines, billboards, radio, television, telephone recordings or other public media.
16. Allows the Underwriting firm to purchase any shares that the issuing company's shareholders have not bought and sell the shares themselves for a profit.
17. A document accompanying or part of a stock certificate that is signed by the person named on the certificate for the purpose of transferring the certificate's title to another person's name.
18. A process that allows industry disputes between members, member organizations, their employees, and customers to be heard and settled by either FINRA or a designated arbitration panel.
19. A market in which buyers enter competitive bids and sellers enter competitive offers simultaneously.

A. Authorized Stock
B. Dealer
C. Standby
D. Current yield
E. Floor Broker
F. Equity income fund
G. Nominal yield
H. Asset Allocation Fund
I. Assignment
J. Advertisement
K. Special Situation Fund
L. Annual return
M. Class A shares
N. Capital Structure
O. Auction Market
P. Accumulation Unit
Q. Annuitant
R. Arbitration
S. Authorized Stock

8.

Find the hidden words. The words have been placed horizontally, vertically, or diagonally. When you locate a word, draw a circle around it.

O	Z	D	M	B	I	D	S	Q	V	P	P	S	Z	E	Y	X	R	O	Q
L	P	Z	X	I	J	V	F	D	A	L	L	O	R	N	O	N	E	B	D
J	K	T	A	N	N	U	I	T	Y	U	N	I	T	N	D	N	F	E	U
E	X	C	H	A	N	G	E	M	A	R	K	E	T	H	Y	K	F	V	R
Q	C	O	N	D	U	I	T	T	H	E	O	R	Y	W	O	Z	T	K	A
V	U	J	C	S	H	A	R	E	S	B	J	J	C	C	T	L	O	G	T
Q	H	G	P	O	L	T	R	A	D	E	D	A	T	E	C	F	W	F	I
W	R	T	E	Q	U	I	T	Y	I	N	C	O	M	E	F	U	N	D	O
T	J	O	U	T	S	T	A	N	D	I	N	G	S	H	A	R	E	S	N
P	F	F	C	O	O	L	I	N	G	O	F	F	P	E	R	I	O	D	T
B	U	Y	J	A	C	C	U	M	U	L	A	T	I	O	N	U	N	I	T
A	I	P	L	K	J	S	H	N	O	M	I	N	A	L	Y	I	E	L	D

1. Traditionally, the 20-day period between the filing date of a registration statement and the effective date of the registration.
2. Growth and income fund
3. Auction market
4. Shares held by the public
5. A type of best efforts underwriting where the entire amount must be sold or the deal is called off.
6. The accounting measure used to determine the amount of each payment to an annuitant during the pay-out period.
7. Coupon, coupon rate, interest
8. Level Load
9. Over the counter. A negotiated market.
10. The price a Market Maker will pay for a security; it's the price an investor would receive if he or she sold the security.
11. An accounting measure used to determine an annuitant's proportionate interest in the insurer's separate account during an annuity's accumulation (deposit) stage.
12. Date transaction is executed.
13. Small cap stocks; maximum capital appreciation; may employ short-term trading strategies; very volatile.
14. Own, Hold, Purchase, Long
15. A theory behind Subchapter M under which distributions to shareholders are not taxed to the investment company.
16. Measure of the bond price in relations to the time the bond end. Taking in consideration the interest-rates, time to maturity, and differences between the coupon rate and the yield to maturity.

A. Accumulation Unit
E. Nominal yield
I. Outstanding shares
M. All or None
B. Annuity Unit
F. Bid
J. Conduit Theory
N. Equity income fund
C. Duration
G. Trade date
K. Cooling off Period
O. Buy
D. Exchange market
H. Aggressive Growth Fund
L. OTC
P. C shares

9. *Find the hidden words. The words have been placed horizontally, vertically, or diagonally. When you locate a word, draw a circle around it.*

G	S	E	T	T	L	E	M	E	N	T	D	A	T	E	A	J	L	B	B
L	D	E	B	E	N	T	U	R	E	Q	X	R	Q	E	P	G	E	R	D
O	A	S	S	E	T	A	L	L	O	C	A	T	I	O	N	F	U	N	D
B	O	A	S	K	P	R	I	C	E	A	N	N	U	I	T	Y	N	A	E
A	A	P	S	P	O	L	I	T	I	C	A	L	R	I	S	K	U	L	D
L	W	I	E	X	D	I	V	I	D	E	N	D	D	A	T	E	B	L	O
F	X	A	W	A	N	N	U	A	L	R	E	T	U	R	N	V	G	O	W
U	D	E	M	M	U	T	U	A	L	F	U	N	D	U	V	P	D	R	V
N	A	G	E	N	C	Y	T	R	A	N	S	A	C	T	I	O	N	N	R
D	Y	B	C	O	N	S	T	A	N	T	D	O	L	L	A	R	S	O	P
M	F	I	F	B	B	O	N	D	H	O	L	D	E	R	X	G	I	N	C
P	G	F	O	S	A	B	A	L	A	N	C	E	D	F	U	N	D	E	B

1. unsecured Bond backed only by the good faith of the corporation. Repayment of the debt is based on the company's promise to repay.
2. A contract between an insurance company and an individual. An annuity generally guarantees lifetime income to the person on whose life the contract is based.
3. Dollars adjusted to show the same purchasing power from one period to another. They are "indexed" for inflation.
4. A transaction in which a broker or dealer acts for the accounts of others by buying or selling securities on behalf of customers.
5. A creditor
6. Date transaction is completed and the seller pays buyer and the buyer receives the shares.
7. Common stock from inside and outside the U.S. Capital appreciation in whatever markets look attractive to manager.
8. Changes in laws or rules may have negative impact on investments. The common wisdom is that political risk is high anytime Congress is in session.
9. A type of mutual fund that at all times some portion of its investment assets in bonds and stocks, creating a balance between the two types of securities.
10. Open end management company.
11. Holding period return
12. A mutual fund that splits its investment assets among stocks, bonds, and other vehicles in an attempt to provide a consistent return for the investor.
13. The date the security trades without its dividends. In order to get a dividend the security needs to be purchased two days prior to the record date or before the ex-dividend date.
14. The price at which the dealer is willing to sell the stock to an investor or another dealer.
15. The stock of normally strong, well-established companies that have demonstrated their ability to pay dividends in good times and bad times.
16. States that the issuing company wants ALL (or nothing) the shares to be sold if not, the underwriting is cancelled.

A. Ex dividend Date
B. Annual return
C. Balanced Fund
D. Debenture
E. Mutual Fund
F. Political Risk
G. Settlement date
H. Annuity
I. Constant dollars
J. Blue Chip Stock
K. Asset Allocation Fund
L. Ask Price
M. All or none
N. Agency Transaction
O. Global Fund
P. Bondholder

10. *Find the hidden words. The words have been placed horizontally, vertically, or diagonally. When you locate a word, draw a circle around it.*

F	A	R	T	I	M	O	N	E	Y	M	A	R	K	E	T	F	U	N	D
L	J	D	U	R	A	T	I	O	N	K	A	M	A	G	E	N	T	M	Q
O	U	A	C	C	R	U	E	D	I	N	T	E	R	E	S	T	S	U	O
O	A	G	E	N	C	Y	B	A	S	I	S	X	U	A	V	C	P	T	A
R	H	V	S	E	T	T	L	E	M	E	N	T	D	A	T	E	R	U	L
B	W	A	M	O	R	T	I	Z	A	T	I	O	N	B	I	D	E	A	L
R	I	N	C	O	M	E	O	B	J	E	C	T	I	V	E	F	M	L	O
O	S	Y	Z	P	Y	C	A	P	I	T	A	L	R	I	S	K	I	F	R
K	E	Q	U	I	T	Y	I	N	C	O	M	E	F	U	N	D	U	U	N
E	T	N	E	T	A	S	S	E	T	V	A	L	U	E	O	A	M	N	O
R	Y	G	F	C	O	C	U	R	R	E	N	C	Y	R	I	S	K	D	N
A	F	F	I	L	I	A	T	E	D	P	E	R	S	O	N	K	B	V	E

1. Measure of the bond price in relations to the time the bond end. Taking in consideration the interest-rates, time to maturity, and differences between the coupon rate and the yield to maturity.
2. Changes in value of a currency versus another currency. Current owners of forign securities may see a negative impact if foreign currency weakens against their home currency.
3. Payment of a debt (principal) over a period of time in periodic installments.
4. An indication of willingness by a trader or dealer to sell a security or a commodity.
5. Buys stocks for its clients and for personal needs based on their listing price on the floor.
6. Investment objective for regular production of cash from investments, through dividend or interest payments. Bonds and preferred stocks are often used to produce income.
7. Dividend paying equities; safe, consistent income with secondary objective of growth; less volatile than other equity funds.
8. Anyone in a position to influence decisions made in a corporation, including officers, directors, principal stockholders, and members of their immediate families.
9. An agency Transaction
10. Principal Risk
11. An individual or a firm that effects securities transactions for the accounts of others.
12. A type of best efforts underwriting where the entire amount must be sold or the deal is called off.
13. Date transaction is completed and the seller pays buyer and the buyer receives the shares.
14. The price of a mutual fund. Calculates to company's funds minus liabilities divided by outstanding shares.
15. The interest that has accumulated since the last interest payment up to, but not including, the settlement date, and that is added to a bond transaction's contract price.
16. The price a Market Maker will pay for a security; it's the price an investor would receive if he or she sold the security.
17. Cash equivalents such as T-bills, CDs, commercial paper, BAs; Preservation of Capital; attempts to maintain $1 NAV ; used to park funds while making investment decisions.
18. Bonds that cost more than the face value.
19. Open end management company.

A. Mutual Fund
E. Accrued Interest
I. Net Asset Value
M. Floor Broker
Q. Income Objective
B. Money Market Fund
F. Duration
J. Bid
N. Agent
R. Agency Basis
C. All or None
G. Capital Risk
K. Amortization
O. Currency Risk
S. Settlement date
D. Equity Income Fund
H. Ask
L. Affiliated Person
P. Premium

11. *Find the hidden words. The words have been placed horizontally, vertically, or diagonally. When you locate a word, draw a circle around it.*

A	F	T	G	C	F	V	O	B	L	U	E	S	K	Y	L	A	W	S	H
A	M	T	F	R	K	B	R	E	A	K	P	O	I	N	T	S	A	L	E
I	P	L	D	H	X	E	B	U	L	L	M	A	R	K	E	T	V	I	S
M	U	T	U	A	L	F	U	N	D	F	A	M	I	L	Y	U	S	L	Q
M	A	O	N	O	N	S	Y	S	T	E	M	A	T	I	C	R	I	S	K
K	S	D	O	P	Z	W	A	L	L	O	R	N	O	N	E	Z	Z	Q	J
A	K	E	T	R	J	D	C	U	R	R	E	N	T	Y	I	E	L	D	R
U	P	A	X	N	L	A	D	V	E	R	T	I	S	E	M	E	N	T	Y
N	R	L	D	D	E	C	L	A	R	A	T	I	O	N	D	A	T	E	Y
F	I	E	K	G	N	H	K	B	U	S	I	N	E	S	S	D	A	Y	A
V	C	R	L	S	C	O	M	M	O	N	S	T	O	C	K	H	E	T	P
R	E	O	J	B	E	S	T	E	F	F	O	R	T	S	Q	U	U	G	E

1. Family of funds, mutual fund complex
2. The sale of investment company shares in amounts just below the point at which the sales charge is reduced on quantity.
3. The date on which the company declares an upcoming dividend.
4. Allows the firm working for the issuing company to sell its shares the best way they can and are not responsible if shares are not sold.
5. A type of best efforts underwriting where the entire amount must be sold or the deal is called off.
6. A day the New York Stock Exchange is open for business (trading).
7. Selection risk, business risk
8. One who deals in securities as a principal, buying and selling for his own account.
9. The basic stock issued by a corporation representing shares of ownership.
10. Alternative Minimum Tax. The requirement to add the income from tax preference items to income above an indexed level. A method to insure that wealthy persons and corporations pay at least some tax.
11. The price at which the dealer is willing to sell the stock to an investor or another dealer.
12. The yield of the security when bought or sold prior to maturity in the secondary market. Current yield relates current income to the security's current price.
13. Any promotional material designed for use by newspapers, magazines, billboards, radio, television, telephone recordings or other public media.
14. State securities laws.
15. Ad Valorem tax
16. A market in which prices of securities are moving higher or are expected to move higher.
17. Broker-dealer firm primarily on the NASDAQ that opens bids and sells a particular security, taking on the risk of selling that security.
18. Cash equivalents such as T-bills, CDs, commercial paper, BAs; Preservation of Capital; attempts to maintain $1 NAV ; used to park funds while making investment decisions.

A. Business Day
B. Blue Sky Laws
C. Mutual Fund Family
D. Breakpoint Sale
E. Ask Price
F. Non-systematic risk
G. Advertisement
H. Property tax
I. Current Yield
J. AMT
K. All or None
L. Common Stock
M. Market Maker
N. Declaration Date
O. Dealer
P. Bull Market
Q. Money Market Fund
R. Best Efforts

12. *Find the hidden words. The words have been placed horizontally, vertically, or diagonally. When you locate a word, draw a circle around it.*

L	I	Q	U	I	D	I	T	Y	O	B	J	E	C	T	I	V	E	N	L
N	E	B	B	A	N	K	E	R	S	A	C	C	E	P	T	A	N	C	E
A	C	O	L	L	A	T	E	R	A	L	T	R	U	S	T	B	O	N	D
K	B	L	U	E	C	H	I	P	S	T	O	C	K	Z	O	T	C	V	Y
E	F	O	A	G	P	K	P	Q	A	N	N	U	I	T	A	N	T	L	S
D	F	I	F	I	N	S	I	D	E	R	C	O	V	E	R	D	E	L	L
H	Y	C	Z	X	F	P	R	E	P	A	Y	M	E	N	T	R	I	S	K
F	Y	C	A	I	C	A	P	I	T	A	L	G	A	I	N	S	J	S	B
X	U	I	S	F	L	O	N	G	K	E	P	R	E	M	I	U	M	X	F
E	G	X	K	D	C	U	R	R	E	N	T	Y	I	E	L	D	F	C	Y
X	A	F	F	I	L	I	A	T	E	D	P	E	R	S	O	N	X	P	L
A	W	O	J	E	E	U	P	Z	D	B	S	H	A	R	E	S	F	I	X

1. Uncovered
2. Fixed-Income Securities: Possibility that homeowners will prepay mortgages more quickly than expected when interest rates fall.
3. Bank End Load
4. This is a primary need for those who never know when they will need cash quickly.
5. Form of debt backed by stocks and or bonds of another corporation. The collateral is held by a trustee for safekeeping.
6. The stock of normally strong, well-established companies that have demonstrated their ability to pay dividends in good times and bad times.
7. Anyone in a position to influence decisions made in a corporation, including officers, directors, principal stockholders, and members of their immediate families.
8. Over the counter. A negotiated market.
9. To offer
10. Bonds that cost more than the face value.
11. The yield of the security when bought or sold prior to maturity in the secondary market. Current yield relates current income to the security's current price.
12. Control person, affiliate
13. Person who receives an annuity contract's distribution.
14. Educational IRA
15. The long-term gain on an asset hold for a period of longer than 12 months.
16. Buy, bought, hold, or own
17. Essentially a letter of credit from a bank guaranteeing payment of a debt.
18. Mix of equities and bonds.

A. Liquidity Objective
E. Premium
I. Capital Gain
M. Blue Chip Stock
Q. Long

B. Collateral Trust Bond
F. Affiliated Person
J. B shares
N. Growth & Income Fund
R. Coverdell

C. Naked
G. Current Yield
K. Prepayment Risk
O. Insider

D. Annuitant
H. Bankers Acceptance
L. OTC
P. Ask

13.

Find the hidden words. The words have been placed horizontally, vertically, or diagonally. When you locate a word, draw a circle around it.

X	I	R	V	B	R	E	A	K	P	O	I	N	T	S	A	L	E	P	C
C	U	M	U	L	A	T	I	V	E	V	O	T	I	N	G	A	C	A	M
U	D	A	M	O	R	T	I	Z	A	T	I	O	N	I	B	R	S	R	U
A	C	C	R	U	E	D	I	N	T	E	R	E	S	T	V	B	H	V	C
C	R	E	D	I	T	R	I	S	K	U	Z	C	Z	E	K	I	A	A	C
O	T	C	X	D	E	B	E	N	T	U	R	E	R	F	J	T	R	L	L
B	R	O	K	E	R	S	E	C	T	O	R	F	U	N	D	R	E	U	E
B	P	P	B	L	U	E	C	H	I	P	S	T	O	C	K	A	S	E	X
C	A	M	T	A	C	C	O	U	N	T	E	X	E	C	U	T	I	V	E
Y	L	I	Q	U	I	D	I	T	Y	O	B	J	E	C	T	I	V	E	Y
Z	F	W	L	A	P	P	R	E	C	I	A	T	I	O	N	O	D	U	L
U	H	B	A	N	K	E	R	S	A	C	C	E	P	T	A	N	C	E	S

1. The stated value of a security, referring to preferred stocks and bonds that the issuer is willing to pay the investor when the bond matures.
2. The interest that has accumulated since the last interest payment up to, but not including, the settlement date, and that is added to a bond transaction's contract price.
3. The sale of investment company shares in amounts just below the point at which the sales charge is reduced on quantity.
4. A process that allows industry disputes between members, member organizations, their employees, and customers to be heard and settled by either FINRA or a designated arbitration panel.
5. Registered Representative
6. Alternative Minimum Tax. The requirement to add the income from tax preference items to income above an indexed level. A method to insure that wealthy persons and corporations pay at least some tax.
7. A type of shareholder voting in which the number of shares held is multiplied by the number of directors to be elected to determine the number of votes a shareholder may cast.
8. Over the counter. A negotiated market.
9. This is a primary need for those who never know when they will need cash quickly.
10. Payment of a debt (principal) over a period of time in periodic installments.
11. Essentially a letter of credit from a bank guaranteeing payment of a debt.
12. The increase in value of an asset. Sometimes called growth.
13. Common stock from particular industry.
14. Level Load
15. unsecured Bond backed only by the good faith of the corporation. Repayment of the debt is based on the company's promise to repay.
16. Possibility that principal or interest will not be paid.
17. The stock of normally strong, well-established companies that have demonstrated their ability to pay dividends in good times and bad times.
18. The role of a brokerage firm when it acts as an agent for a customer and charges the customer a commission for its services.

A. C shares
B. Par Value
C. Broker
D. OTC
E. Sector Fund
F. Breakpoint Sale
G. Blue Chip Stock
H. Bankers Acceptance
I. Account Executive
J. Appreciation
K. Cumulative Voting
L. Accrued Interest
M. Credit Risk
N. Debenture
O. Arbitration
P. Liquidity Objective
Q. AMT
R. Amortization

14. *Find the hidden words. The words have been placed horizontally, vertically, or diagonally. When you locate a word, draw a circle around it.*

U	A	N	N	U	I	T	Y	B	R	O	K	E	R	U	N	B	K	V	M
C	A	L	L	P	R	I	C	E	B	E	A	R	M	A	R	K	E	T	Z
T	I	M	I	N	G	R	I	S	K	Y	V	F	A	G	D	I	K	Y	K
F	C	O	N	D	U	I	T	T	H	E	O	R	Y	O	L	Z	V	X	D
O	D	A	U	C	T	I	O	N	M	A	R	K	E	T	S	R	W	K	Z
I	Q	Y	B	A	L	A	N	C	E	D	F	U	N	D	L	O	X	D	R
U	C	A	C	C	U	M	U	L	A	T	I	O	N	S	T	A	G	E	X
D	D	S	A	M	O	R	T	I	Z	A	T	I	O	N	Z	Z	S	C	S
W	A	P	S	H	U	P	A	Y	M	E	N	T	D	A	T	E	Z	Q	Y
S	P	E	C	I	A	L	S	I	T	U	A	T	I	O	N	F	U	N	D
W	L	I	Q	U	I	D	I	T	Y	R	I	S	K	R	V	D	O	W	X
K	H	S	U	I	N	D	E	X	F	U	N	D	M	V	T	K	M	N	V

1. A market where sellers bid for stock and buyers sell their stock.
2. Equity Category; Portfolio: common stock in same proportions as selected index.
3. Payment of a debt (principal) over a period of time in periodic installments.
4. Investing in a specific security at an inopportune time. Dollar cost averaging is used to avoid this risk.
5. Possible large gain if situation plays out as manager predicts; Depends on ability of manager to find special deals.
6. A theory behind Subchapter M under which distributions to shareholders are not taxed to the investment company.
7. The date the company mails out the dividend.
8. The role of a brokerage firm when it acts as an agent for a customer and charges the customer a commission for its services.
9. Mix of equities and bonds; growth with opportunity for income; portfolio mix usually under tighter constraints than growth & income fund.
10. Ability to quickly sell an investment at or near current market price. Regardless of type, more heavily traded securities are more liquid.
11. The period during which contributions are made to an annuity account.
12. A market in which prices of securities are falling or are expected to fall.
13. Front end sales charge, front end load
14. The price paid for callable preferred stock or bonds redeemed by the issuer prior to maturity of the issue because interest rates have fallen.
15. An accounting measure used to determine the amount of each payment during an annuity's distribution stage.
16. A contract between an insurance company and an individual, generally guaranteeing lifetime income to the individual.
17. Wholesaler, sponsor, underwriter

A. Annuity Unit
B. Broker
C. Class A shares
D. Index Fund
E. Balanced Fund
F. Payment date
G. Call Price
H. Auction markets
I. Distributor
J. Bear Market
K. Conduit Theory
L. Annuity
M. Special Situation Fund
N. Amortization
O. Accumulation Stage
P. Timing Risk
Q. Liquidity Risk

15. *Find the hidden words. The words have been placed horizontally, vertically, or diagonally. When you locate a word, draw a circle around it.*

S	E	D	O	C	O	N	T	R	A	C	T	U	A	L	P	L	A	N	K
P	D	C	N	Y	S	X	B	R	Q	A	L	L	O	R	N	O	N	E	P
G	E	O	V	C	B	R	E	A	K	P	O	I	N	T	S	A	L	E	H
D	A	R	N	E	T	A	S	S	E	T	V	A	L	U	E	U	P	G	V
E	L	P	P	D	R	A	T	B	A	L	A	N	C	E	D	F	U	N	D
A	L	O	I	U	F	B	E	G	F	F	U	Y	H	M	U	H	G	F	Z
L	O	R	A	R	X	F	F	M	M	U	T	U	A	L	F	U	N	D	Q
E	R	A	B	A	E	G	F	Q	Y	G	L	O	B	A	L	F	U	N	D
R	N	T	H	T	F	S	O	A	G	L	J	O	X	A	S	S	E	T	K
G	O	I	X	I	M	R	R	M	N	R	X	R	H	U	J	O	W	B	V
O	N	O	J	O	P	C	T	T	B	Y	A	N	N	U	I	T	Y	D	Z
K	E	N	I	N	X	A	S	A	N	N	U	A	L	R	E	T	U	R	N

1. Mix of equities and bonds; growth with opportunity for income; portfolio mix usually under tighter constraints than growth & income fund.
2. Allows the firm working for the issuing company to sell its shares the best way they can and are not responsible if shares are not sold.
3. The sale of investment company shares in amounts just below the point at which the sales charge is reduced on quantity.
4. The price of a mutual fund. Calculates to company's funds minus liabilities divided by outstanding shares.
5. A form of business organization in which the total worth of the organization is divided into shares of stock.
6. Alternative Minimum Tax. The requirement to add the income from tax preference items to income above an indexed level. A method to insure that wealthy persons and corporations pay at least some tax.
7. States that the issuing company wants ALL (or nothing) the shares to be sold if not, the underwriting is cancelled.
8. Possible large gain if situation plays out as manager predicts; Depends on ability of manager to find special deals.
9. Common stock from inside and outside the U.S. Capital appreciation in whatever markets look attractive to manager.
10. Open end management company.
11. Measure of the bond price in relations to the time the bond end. Taking in consideration the interest-rates, time to maturity, and differences between the coupon rate and the yield to maturity.
12. Principal
13. Holding period return
14. Also called period payment plans.
15. A type of best efforts underwriting where the entire amount must be sold or the deal is called off.
16. Anything that an individual or a corporation owns.
17. A contract between an insurance company and an individual. An annuity generally guarantees lifetime income to the person on whose life the contract is based.

A. Balanced Fund
B. Duration
C. Net Asset Value
D. Mutual Fund
E. Special Situation Fund
F. Asset
G. Corporation
H. Global Fund
I. Best Efforts
J. All or none
K. Annuity
L. All or None
M. Breakpoint Sale
N. Dealer
O. Contractual Plan
P. Annual return
Q. AMT

1. *Find the hidden words. The words have been placed horizontally, vertically, or diagonally. When you locate a word, draw a circle around it.*

Q	N	U	A	S	K	P	R	I	C	E	G	X	H	L	L	O	N	G	Y
L	I	Q	U	I	D	I	T	Y	R	I	S	K	H	C	M	O	M	S	E
V	K	W	A	C	R	E	D	I	T	R	I	S	K	L	G	M	O	D	O
A	D	K	R	I	N	V	E	S	T	M	E	N	T	I	N	C	O	M	E
E	A	L	L	O	R	N	O	N	E	U	B	U	Y	M	G	B	D	W	W
H	Q	H	S	S	M	A	R	K	E	T	R	I	S	K	D	I	K	V	M
R	T	I	M	I	N	G	R	I	S	K	K	C	K	Z	O	D	V	H	P
H	P	R	O	G	R	E	S	S	I	V	E	T	A	X	E	P	Y	Q	S
W	C	L	A	S	S	A	S	H	A	R	E	S	E	A	A	R	G	C	H
C	O	M	M	O	N	S	T	O	C	K	A	H	I	S	W	I	H	N	T
P	H	A	G	E	N	C	Y	B	A	S	I	S	S	K	C	C	B	T	R
W	P	A	A	A	P	P	R	E	C	I	A	T	I	O	N	E	R	Q	Y

1. interest & dividends
2. Buy, bought, hold, or own
3. Ability to quickly sell an investment at or near current market price. Regardless of type, more heavily traded securities are more liquid.
4. To offer
5. Investing in a specific security at an inopportune time. Dollar cost averaging is used to avoid this risk.
6. Possibility that principal or interest will not be paid.
7. The price at which a dealer is willing to buy stock from an individual or another dealer.
8. The basic stock issued by a corporation representing shares of ownership.
9. Systematic risk
10. The increase in value of an asset. Sometimes called growth.
11. An agency Transaction
12. The price at which the dealer is willing to sell the stock to an investor or another dealer.
13. Front end sales charge, front end load
14. Graduated tax, income tax
15. States that the issuing company wants ALL (or nothing) the shares to be sold if not, the underwriting is cancelled.
16. The accounting measure used to determine the amount of each payment to an annuitant during the pay-out period.
17. Own, Hold, Purchase, Long

A. Progressive tax
B. Liquidity Risk
C. Investment income
D. Market risk
E. Timing Risk
F. Ask
G. Bid Price
H. Ask Price
I. Buy
J. Appreciation
K. Common Stock
L. Credit Risk
M. Annuity Unit
N. Agency Basis
O. All or none
P. Class A shares
Q. Long

2. *Find the hidden words. The words have been placed horizontally, vertically, or diagonally. When you locate a word, draw a circle around it.*

M	U	T	U	A	L	F	U	N	D	F	A	M	I	L	Y	F	R	M	W
A	U	C	T	I	O	N	M	A	R	K	E	T	S	R	X	Q	Y	U	K
O	R	I	N	D	E	X	F	U	N	D	W	A	M	T	H	B	N	T	M
J	C	A	P	P	R	E	C	I	A	T	I	O	N	G	C	R	L	U	D
C	U	M	U	L	A	T	I	V	E	V	O	T	I	N	G	O	V	A	E
D	E	C	L	A	R	A	T	I	O	N	D	A	T	E	F	K	Z	L	B
C	O	O	L	I	N	G	O	F	F	P	E	R	I	O	D	E	W	F	E
C	U	R	R	E	N	T	D	O	L	L	A	R	S	E	C	R	F	U	N
Z	V	H	D	A	G	E	N	C	Y	D	E	B	T	A	P	M	I	N	T
U	Q	M	M	O	N	E	Y	M	A	R	K	E	T	F	U	N	D	D	U
E	A	C	C	R	U	E	D	I	N	T	E	R	E	S	T	K	W	V	R
F	T	L	O	N	G	A	S	P	R	E	A	D	A	V	E	R	A	G	E

1. Often called "Indirect Debt."
2. An agent
3. Alternative Minimum Tax. The requirement to add the income from tax preference items to income above an indexed level. A method to insure that wealthy persons and corporations pay at least some tax.
4. Actual dollar amounts. Not adjusted for inflation.
5. The date on which the company declares an upcoming dividend.
6. The interest that has accumulated since the last interest payment up to, but not including, the settlement date, and that is added to a bond transaction's contract price.
7. A price at a midpoint among a number of prices. Technical analysts often use averages as market indicators.
8. Family of funds, mutual fund complex
9. Traditionally, the 20-day period between the filing date of a registration statement and the effective date of the registration.
10. Equity Category; Portfolio: common stock in same proportions as selected index.
11. The increase in value of an asset. Sometimes called growth.
12. A type of shareholder voting in which the number of shares held is multiplied by the number of directors to be elected to determine the number of votes a shareholder may cast.
13. unsecured Bond backed only by the good faith of the corporation. Repayment of the debt is based on the company's promise to repay.
14. Buy, bought, hold, or own
15. Cash equivalents such as T-bills, CDs, commercial paper, BAs; Preservation of Capital; attempts to maintain $1 NAV ; used to park funds while making investment decisions.
16. Open end management company.
17. Is the price difference the Market Maker is willing to buy the stock for, to the amount he
18. Any institution or an individual meeting minimum net worth requirements for the purchase of securities qualifying under the Regulation D registration exemption.
19. A market where sellers bid for stock and buyers sell their stock.

A. Index Fund	B. Average
E. AMT	F. Accrued Interest
I. Mutual Fund Family	J. Auction markets
M. Broker	N. Appreciation
Q. Debenture	R. Accredited Investor

C. Cumulative Voting	D. Current Dollars
G. Money Market Fund	H. Long
K. Agency Debt	L. Mutual Fund
O. Declaration Date	P. Cooling off Period
S. Spread	

3. *Find the hidden words. The words have been placed horizontally, vertically, or diagonally. When you locate a word, draw a circle around it.*

F	T	G	F	E	X	D	I	V	I	D	E	N	D	D	A	T	E	G	M
N	I	N	T	E	R	N	A	T	I	O	N	A	L	F	U	N	D	L	U
X	G	I	N	V	E	S	T	M	E	N	T	B	A	N	K	E	R	O	U
S	F	B	I	D	V	R	O	S	R	D	E	A	L	E	R	C	C	B	K
R	H	V	E	B	A	L	A	N	C	E	D	F	U	N	D	R	T	A	Q
C	R	E	D	I	T	R	I	S	K	B	S	O	A	A	G	V	Z	L	J
Z	C	A	P	I	T	A	L	S	T	R	U	C	T	U	R	E	T	F	J
U	N	E	T	A	S	S	E	T	V	A	L	U	E	J	C	I	R	U	P
O	A	U	T	H	O	R	I	Z	E	D	S	T	O	C	K	U	U	N	P
R	F	M	U	N	I	C	I	P	A	L	B	O	N	D	F	U	N	D	S
C	I	D	E	C	L	A	R	A	T	I	O	N	D	A	T	E	J	X	Y
B	N	B	A	C	K	E	N	D	S	A	L	E	S	C	H	A	R	G	E

1. Income that is free from federal, and possibly state income tax; higher the investor's tax bracket, the more beneficial the tax exemption; may have some default risk; interest rate risk.
2. Common stock from inside and outside the U.S. Capital appreciation in whatever markets look attractive to manager.
3. The price a Market Maker will pay for a security; it's the price an investor would receive if he or she sold the security.
4. The amount of debt or equity issued by a corporation.
5. Principal
6. Common stocks from outside of the U.S.; Exposure to exchange rate risk and political (legistlative) risk, in addition to market risk.
7. Mix of equities and bonds; growth with opportunity for income; portfolio mix usually under tighter constraints than growth & income fund.
8. "New" stock
9. The date on which the company declares an upcoming dividend.
10. Contingent deferred sales charge (CDSC)
11. Default risk
12. Introduces new securities to the market, that advises the issuing company of the price the security will be sold for to the public.
13. The price of a mutual fund. Calculates to company's funds minus liabilities divided by outstanding shares.
14. The date the security trades without its dividends. In order to get a dividend the security needs to be purchased two days prior to the record date or before the ex-dividend date.
15. A base for illustrating payments from a variable annuity.
16. The stock of normally strong, well-established companies that have demonstrated their ability to pay dividends in good times and bad times.
17. A theory behind Subchapter M under which distributions to shareholders are not taxed to the investment company.
18. Investment objective for investors that are willing and able to take considerable risks for the chance to hit a big financial home run.

A. Back end sales charge
B. Speculation Objective
C. International Fund
D. Balanced Fund
E. Blue Chip Stock
F. Capital Structure
G. Credit risk
H. Conduit Theory
I. Authorized stock
J. Ex dividend Date
K. Bid
L. Municipal Bond Fund
M. Global Fund
N. Investment Banker
O. Net Asset Value
P. Assumed Interest Rate
Q. Dealer
R. Declaration Date

4. *Find the hidden words. The words have been placed horizontally, vertically, or diagonally. When you locate a word, draw a circle around it.*

S	X	S	F	R	U	S	Z	C	U	S	T	O	D	I	A	N	Z	S	F
S	P	E	C	I	A	L	S	I	T	U	A	T	I	O	N	F	U	N	D
T	X	T	I	I	N	C	O	M	E	O	B	J	E	C	T	I	V	E	B
O	Y	D	O	C	A	C	C	R	U	E	D	I	N	T	E	R	E	S	T
Y	V	M	A	C	A	L	L	P	R	O	V	I	S	I	O	N	S	J	H
Y	X	M	C	O	S	T	B	A	S	I	S	C	K	X	F	Q	W	Q	X
R	W	X	P	G	R	O	W	T	H	O	B	J	E	C	T	I	V	E	V
B	J	A	L	L	O	R	N	O	N	E	A	N	N	U	I	T	I	Z	E
Y	C	R	E	D	I	T	R	I	S	K	E	X	C	H	A	N	G	E	H
Z	T	C	O	N	D	U	I	T	T	H	E	O	R	Y	H	U	Y	U	M
C	O	U	P	O	N	R	A	T	E	R	E	C	O	R	D	A	T	E
L	C	O	N	V	E	R	T	I	B	L	E	B	O	N	D	U	B	G	F

1. Investment objective for regular production of cash from investments, through dividend or interest payments. Bonds and preferred stocks are often used to produce income.
2. Possibility that principal or interest will not be paid.
3. Switch
4. A theory behind Subchapter M under which distributions to shareholders are not taxed to the investment company.
5. The Investment Company Act of 1940 requires the fund's assets be held by an independent custodian.
6. Possible large gain if situation plays out as manager predicts; Depends on ability of manager to find special deals.
7. Nominal Yield
8. A bond that may be exchanged for some other security of the issuer at the option of the holder. It is usually converted into common stock based upon a fixed conversion ratio.
9. The interest that has accumulated since the last interest payment up to, but not including, the settlement date, and that is added to a bond transaction's contract price.
10. Investment objective for increase in invested capital, primarily generated through price appreciation. Equity securities (stocks) are usually used in pursuit of this goal.
11. An issuing corporation retains the privilege of recalling (redeeming) its issues of equity or debt.
12. States that the issuing company wants ALL (or nothing) the shares to be sold if not, the underwriting is cancelled.
13. To change an annuity contract from the accumulation (pay-in) stage to the distribution (payout) stage.
14. A debt security issued by an authorized agency of the federal government.
15. Registered Representative
16. Money on which taxes have been paid. A return of cost basis is a return of capital and not subject to tax.
17. Date where the BOD checks if a shareholder is listed with the company, so they can get paid their dividends.
18. Principal Risk

A. Credit Risk
E. Income Objective
I. Account Executive
M. Convertible Bond
Q. All or none

B. Coupon Rate
F. Special Situation Fund
J. Growth Objective
N. Conduit Theory
R. Call Provisions

C. Annuitize
G. Capital Risk
K. Agency Issue
O. Accrued Interest

D. Cost Basis
H. Exchange
L. Record Date
P. Custodian

5. *Find the hidden words. The words have been placed horizontally, vertically, or diagonally. When you locate a word, draw a circle around it.*

I	N	C	O	D	E	O	F	A	R	B	I	T	R	A	T	I	O	N	S
D	E	B	E	N	T	U	R	E	S	E	C	T	O	R	F	U	N	D	T
C	B	A	C	K	E	N	D	S	A	L	E	S	C	H	A	R	G	E	S
C	A	G	E	N	C	Y	D	E	B	T	N	P	V	V	S	C	M	L	T
A	R	H	S	H	Q	C	O	N	T	R	I	B	U	T	I	O	N	N	A
L	D	U	P	S	P	E	C	I	A	L	I	S	T	C	B	C	I	F	N
L	P	R	R	E	A	N	N	U	A	L	R	E	T	U	R	N	Q	A	D
R	K	U	E	W	V	J	S	J	A	N	N	U	I	T	A	N	T	S	B
I	J	E	M	A	D	V	E	R	T	I	S	E	M	E	N	T	S	Y
S	H	M	D	O	D	P	A	U	C	T	I	O	N	M	A	R	K	E	T
K	W	H	W	B	R	E	A	K	P	O	I	N	T	S	A	L	E	T	C
Q	N	W	X	Q	H	A	U	C	T	I	O	N	M	A	R	K	E	T	S

1. Allows the Underwriting firm to purchase any shares that the issuing company's shareholders have not bought and sell the shares themselves for a profit.
2. Is the price difference the Market Maker is willing to buy the stock for, to the amount he
3. A market where sellers bid for stock and buyers sell their stock.
4. A stock exchange where the securities are sold to the highest bidder.
5. Anything that an individual or a corporation owns.
6. Holding period return
7. The sale of investment company shares in amounts just below the point at which the sales charge is reduced on quantity.
8. Bonds are more likely to be called when rates have dropped, forcing reinvestment of principal at lower rates.
9. Often called "Indirect Debt."
10. Any promotional material designed for use by newspapers, magazines, billboards, radio, television, telephone recordings or other public media.
11. Cost basis
12. Common stock from particular industry.
13. Provides a method of handling securities-related disputes or clearing controversies between members, public customers, clearing corporations or clearing banks.
14. Person who receives an annuity contract's distribution.
15. unsecured Bond backed only by the good faith of the corporation. Repayment of the debt is based on the company's promise to repay.
16. Auctioneer of the stock, sets the opening bid, facilitates the trade between brokers and dealers, and makes sure the best bid for the stock is executed and sold.
17. Contingent deferred sales charge (CDSC)
18. The stock of normally strong, well-established companies that have demonstrated their ability to pay dividends in good times and bad times.

A. Code of Arbitrations
B. Sector Fund
C. Advertisement
D. Asset
E. Back end sales charge
F. Auction Market
G. Spread
H. Specialist
I. Annual return
J. Breakpoint Sale
K. Auction markets
L. Call Risk
M. Standby
N. Debenture
O. Blue Chip Stock
P. Annuitant
Q. Agency Debt
R. Contribution

6. *Find the hidden words. The words have been placed horizontally, vertically, or diagonally. When you locate a word, draw a circle around it.*

E	D	G	F	A	O	M	V	M	A	R	B	I	T	R	A	T	I	O	N
L	E	K	T	G	X	G	Q	A	B	U	S	I	N	E	S	S	D	A	Y
A	G	I	I	E	B	C	U	R	R	E	N	T	Y	I	E	L	D	Z	Y
X	M	B	M	N	W	H	N	K	Y	C	R	E	D	I	T	R	I	S	K
M	L	X	I	T	T	P	N	E	C	O	X	F	O	E	O	D	D	P	Z
L	A	J	N	P	O	L	I	T	I	C	A	L	R	I	S	K	S	R	P
Q	U	C	G	S	P	J	W	V	I	N	C	O	M	E	B	O	N	D	U
Z	R	E	R	T	B	A	L	A	N	C	E	D	F	U	N	D	T	Q	T
M	U	N	I	C	I	P	A	L	B	O	N	D	S	G	Y	C	V	Z	B
C	W	A	S	K	E	D	K	U	V	T	R	A	D	E	D	A	T	E
W	B	K	K	A	P	P	R	E	C	I	A	T	I	O	N	H	D	F	U
W	H	Y	M	C	R	E	D	I	T	R	I	S	K	V	M	F	B	L	O

1. Current bid and asking price of security.
2. Changes in laws or rules may have negative impact on investments. The common wisdom is that political risk is high anytime Congress is in session.
3. Present yield the buyer would receive when purchasing the bond. Calculated by dividing Annual Interest rates to Market Price.
4. Tax-free bonds
5. Investing in a specific security at an inopportune time. Dollar cost averaging is used to avoid this risk.
6. Date transaction is executed.
7. Default risk
8. Mix of equities and bonds; growth with opportunity for income; portfolio mix usually under tighter constraints than growth & income fund.
9. A process that allows industry disputes between members, member organizations, their employees, and customers to be heard and settled by either FINRA or a designated arbitration panel.
10. A day the New York Stock Exchange is open for business (trading).
11. Adjusted Gross Income. Earned income plus net passive income, portfolio income, and capital gains.
12. Adjustment bond
13. An individual or a firm that effects securities transactions for the accounts of others.
14. The increase in value of an asset. Sometimes called growth.
15. Possibility that principal or interest will not be paid.
16. This is the price an investor would pay when buying the security.

A. Agent
F. Business Day
K. AGI
P. Appreciation

B. Income bond
G. Balanced Fund
L. Credit Risk

C. Political Risk
H. Arbitration
M. Market Value

D. Current yield
I. Timing Risk
N. Credit risk

E. Municipal bonds
J. Trade date
O. Asked

7. Find the hidden words. The words have been placed horizontally, vertically, or diagonally. When you locate a word, draw a circle around it.

N	A	S	S	E	T	A	L	L	O	C	A	T	I	O	N	F	U	N	D
K	J	K	Y	G	C	L	A	S	S	A	S	H	A	R	E	S	E	C	H
X	R	S	T	A	N	D	B	Y	N	N	N	X	D	E	A	L	E	R	R
W	V	M	E	Q	U	I	T	Y	I	N	C	O	M	E	F	U	N	D	U
C	A	P	I	T	A	L	S	T	R	U	C	T	U	R	E	J	R	O	Y
Y	X	J	U	U	C	P	N	O	M	I	N	A	L	Y	I	E	L	D	Q
Y	Q	A	C	C	U	M	U	L	A	T	I	O	N	U	N	I	T	N	J
A	S	S	I	G	N	M	E	N	T	A	A	L	J	Y	V	F	F	V	I
C	I	T	B	U	Y	R	S	A	N	N	U	A	L	R	E	T	U	R	N
H	B	X	Y	L	A	D	V	E	R	T	I	S	E	M	E	N	T	L	M
P	M	K	A	U	T	H	O	R	I	Z	E	D	S	T	O	C	K	Z	S
G	T	X	C	U	R	R	E	N	T	Y	I	E	L	D	A	N	R	L	M

1. Present yield the buyer would receive when purchasing the bond. Calculated by dividing Annual Interest rates to Market Price.
2. The annuity contract holder.
3. A mutual fund that splits its investment assets among stocks, bonds, and other vehicles in an attempt to provide a consistent return for the investor.
4. Authorized stock is the maximum number of shares a corporation may issue under the terms of its charter.
5. The amount of debt or equity issued by a corporation.
6. Growth and income fund
7. Possible large gain if situation plays out as manager predicts; Depends on ability of manager to find special deals.
8. Front end sales charge, front end load
9. Principal
10. Holding period return
11. The number of shares of stock that a corporation may issue.
12. Coupon, coupon rate, interest
13. Buys stocks for its clients and for personal needs based on their listing price on the floor.
14. An accounting measure used to determine an annuitant's proportionate interest in the insurer's separate account during an annuity's accumulation (deposit) stage.
15. Any promotional material designed for use by newspapers, magazines, billboards, radio, television, telephone recordings or other public media.
16. Allows the Underwriting firm to purchase any shares that the issuing company's shareholders have not bought and sell the shares themselves for a profit.
17. A document accompanying or part of a stock certificate that is signed by the person named on the certificate for the purpose of transferring the certificate's title to another person's name.
18. A process that allows industry disputes between members, member organizations, their employees, and customers to be heard and settled by either FINRA or a designated arbitration panel.
19. A market in which buyers enter competitive bids and sellers enter competitive offers simultaneously.

A. Authorized Stock
B. Dealer
C. Standby
D. Current yield
E. Floor Broker
F. Equity income fund
G. Nominal yield
H. Asset Allocation Fund
I. Assignment
J. Advertisement
K. Special Situation Fund
L. Annual return
M. Class A shares
N. Capital Structure
O. Auction Market
P. Accumulation Unit
Q. Annuitant
R. Arbitration
S. Authorized Stock

8. *Find the hidden words. The words have been placed horizontally, vertically, or diagonally. When you locate a word, draw a circle around it.*

O	Z	D	M	B	I	D	S	Q	V	P	P	S	Z	E	Y	X	R	O	Q
L	P	Z	X	I	J	V	F	D	A	L	L	O	R	N	O	N	E	B	D
J	K	T	A	N	N	U	I	T	Y	U	N	I	T	N	D	N	F	E	U
E	X	C	H	A	N	G	E	M	A	R	K	E	T	H	Y	K	F	V	R
Q	C	O	N	D	U	I	T	T	H	E	O	R	Y	W	O	Z	T	K	A
V	U	J	C	S	H	A	R	E	S	B	J	J	C	C	T	L	O	G	T
Q	H	G	P	O	L	T	R	A	D	E	D	A	T	E	C	F	W	F	I
W	R	T	E	Q	U	I	T	Y	I	N	C	O	M	E	F	U	N	D	O
T	J	O	U	T	S	T	A	N	D	I	N	G	S	H	A	R	E	S	N
P	F	F	C	O	O	L	I	N	G	O	F	F	P	E	R	I	O	D	T
B	U	Y	J	A	C	C	U	M	U	L	A	T	I	O	N	U	N	I	T
A	I	P	L	K	J	S	H	N	O	M	I	N	A	L	Y	I	E	L	D

1. Traditionally, the 20-day period between the filing date of a registration statement and the effective date of the registration.
2. Growth and income fund
3. Auction market
4. Shares held by the public
5. A type of best efforts underwriting where the entire amount must be sold or the deal is called off.
6. The accounting measure used to determine the amount of each payment to an annuitant during the pay-out period.
7. Coupon, coupon rate, interest
8. Level Load
9. Over the counter. A negotiated market.
10. The price a Market Maker will pay for a security; it's the price an investor would receive if he or she sold the security.
11. An accounting measure used to determine an annuitant's proportionate interest in the insurer's separate account during an annuity's accumulation (deposit) stage.
12. Date transaction is executed.
13. Small cap stocks; maximum capital appreciation; may employ short-term trading strategies; very volatile.
14. Own, Hold, Purchase, Long
15. A theory behind Subchapter M under which distributions to shareholders are not taxed to the investment company.
16. Measure of the bond price in relations to the time the bond end. Taking in consideration the interest-rates, time to maturity, and differences between the coupon rate and the yield to maturity.

A. Accumulation Unit
E. Nominal yield
I. Outstanding shares
M. All or None

B. Annuity Unit
F. Bid
J. Conduit Theory
N. Equity income fund

C. Duration
G. Trade date
K. Cooling off Period
O. Buy

D. Exchange market
H. Aggressive Growth Fund
L. OTC
P. C shares

9. *Find the hidden words. The words have been placed horizontally, vertically, or diagonally. When you locate a word, draw a circle around it.*

G	S	E	T	T	L	E	M	E	N	T	D	A	T	E	A	J	L	B	B
L	D	E	B	E	N	T	U	R	E	Q	X	R	Q	E	P	G	E	R	D
O	A	S	S	E	T	A	L	L	O	C	A	T	I	O	N	F	U	N	D
B	O	A	S	K	P	R	I	C	E	A	N	N	U	I	T	Y	N	A	E
A	A	P	S	P	O	L	I	T	I	C	A	L	R	I	S	K	U	L	D
L	W	I	E	X	D	I	V	I	D	E	N	D	D	A	T	E	B	L	O
F	X	A	W	A	N	N	U	A	L	R	E	T	U	R	N	V	G	O	W
U	D	E	M	M	U	T	U	A	L	F	U	N	D	U	V	P	D	R	V
N	A	G	E	N	C	Y	T	R	A	N	S	A	C	T	I	O	N	N	R
D	Y	B	C	O	N	S	T	A	N	T	D	O	L	L	A	R	S	O	P
M	F	I	F	B	B	O	N	D	H	O	L	D	E	R	X	G	I	N	C
P	G	F	O	S	A	B	A	L	A	N	C	E	D	F	U	N	D	E	B

1. unsecured Bond backed only by the good faith of the corporation. Repayment of the debt is based on the company's promise to repay.
2. A contract between an insurance company and an individual. An annuity generally guarantees lifetime income to the person on whose life the contract is based.
3. Dollars adjusted to show the same purchasing power from one period to another. They are "indexed" for inflation.
4. A transaction in which a broker or dealer acts for the accounts of others by buying or selling securities on behalf of customers.
5. A creditor
6. Date transaction is completed and the seller pays buyer and the buyer receives the shares.
7. Common stock from inside and outside the U.S. Capital appreciation in whatever markets look attractive to manager.
8. Changes in laws or rules may have negative impact on investments. The common wisdom is that political risk is high anytime Congress is in session.
9. A type of mutual fund that at all times some portion of its investment assets in bonds and stocks, creating a balance between the two types of securities.
10. Open end management company.
11. Holding period return
12. A mutual fund that splits its investment assets among stocks, bonds, and other vehicles in an attempt to provide a consistent return for the investor.
13. The date the security trades without its dividends. In order to get a dividend the security needs to be purchased two days prior to the record date or before the ex-dividend date.
14. The price at which the dealer is willing to sell the stock to an investor or another dealer.
15. The stock of normally strong, well-established companies that have demonstrated their ability to pay dividends in good times and bad times.
16. States that the issuing company wants ALL (or nothing) the shares to be sold if not, the underwriting is cancelled.

A. Ex dividend Date
B. Annual return
C. Balanced Fund
D. Debenture
E. Mutual Fund
F. Political Risk
G. Settlement date
H. Annuity
I. Constant dollars
J. Blue Chip Stock
K. Asset Allocation Fund
L. Ask Price
M. All or none
N. Agency Transaction
O. Global Fund
P. Bondholder

10. *Find the hidden words. The words have been placed horizontally, vertically, or diagonally. When you locate a word, draw a circle around it.*

F	A	R	T	I	M	O	N	E	Y	M	A	R	K	E	T	F	U	N	D
L	J	D	U	R	A	T	I	O	N	K	A	M	A	G	E	N	T	M	Q
O	U	A	C	C	R	U	E	D	I	N	T	E	R	E	S	T	S	U	O
O	A	G	E	N	C	Y	B	A	S	I	S	X	U	A	V	C	P	T	A
R	H	V	S	E	T	T	L	E	M	E	N	T	D	A	T	E	R	U	L
B	W	A	M	O	R	T	I	Z	A	T	I	O	N	B	I	D	E	A	L
R	I	N	C	O	M	E	O	B	J	E	C	T	I	V	E	F	M	L	O
O	S	Y	Z	P	Y	C	A	P	I	T	A	L	R	I	S	K	I	F	R
K	E	Q	U	I	T	Y	I	N	C	O	M	E	F	U	N	D	U	U	N
E	T	N	E	T	A	S	S	E	T	V	A	L	U	E	O	A	M	N	O
R	Y	G	F	C	O	C	U	R	R	E	N	C	Y	R	I	S	K	D	N
A	F	F	I	L	I	A	T	E	D	P	E	R	S	O	N	K	B	V	E

1. Measure of the bond price in relations to the time the bond end. Taking in consideration the interest-rates, time to maturity, and differences between the coupon rate and the yield to maturity.
2. Changes in value of a currency versus another currency. Current owners of forign securities may see a negative impact if foreign currency weakens against their home currency.
3. Payment of a debt (principal) over a period of time in periodic installments.
4. An indication of willingness by a trader or dealer to sell a security or a commodity.
5. Buys stocks for its clients and for personal needs based on their listing price on the floor.
6. Investment objective for regular production of cash from investments, through dividend or interest payments. Bonds and preferred stocks are often used to produce income.
7. Dividend paying equities; safe, consistent income with secondary objective of growth; less volatile than other equity funds.
8. Anyone in a position to influence decisions made in a corporation, including officers, directors, principal stockholders, and members of their immediate families.
9. An agency Transaction
10. Principal Risk
11. An individual or a firm that effects securities transactions for the accounts of others.
12. A type of best efforts underwriting where the entire amount must be sold or the deal is called off.
13. Date transaction is completed and the seller pays buyer and the buyer receives the shares.
14. The price of a mutual fund. Calculates to company's funds minus liabilities divided by outstanding shares.
15. The interest that has accumulated since the last interest payment up to, but not including, the settlement date, and that is added to a bond transaction's contract price.
16. The price a Market Maker will pay for a security; it's the price an investor would receive if he or she sold the security.
17. Cash equivalents such as T-bills, CDs, commercial paper, BAs; Preservation of Capital; attempts to maintain $1 NAV ; used to park funds while making investment decisions.
18. Bonds that cost more than the face value.
19. Open end management company.

A. Mutual Fund
E. Accrued Interest
I. Net Asset Value
M. Floor Broker
Q. Income Objective

B. Money Market Fund
F. Duration
J. Bid
N. Agent
R. Agency Basis

C. All or None
G. Capital Risk
K. Amortization
O. Currency Risk
S. Settlement date

D. Equity Income Fund
H. Ask
L. Affiliated Person
P. Premium

11. *Find the hidden words. The words have been placed horizontally, vertically, or diagonally. When you locate a word, draw a circle around it.*

A	F	T	G	C	F	V	O	B	L	U	E	S	K	Y	L	A	W	S	H
A	M	T	F	R	K	B	R	E	A	K	P	O	I	N	T	S	A	L	E
I	P	L	D	H	X	E	B	U	L	L	M	A	R	K	E	T	V	I	S
M	U	T	U	A	L	F	U	N	D	F	A	M	I	L	Y	U	S	L	Q
M	A	O	N	O	N	S	Y	S	T	E	M	A	T	I	C	R	I	S	K
K	S	D	O	P	Z	W	A	L	L	O	R	N	O	N	E	Z	Z	Q	J
A	K	E	T	R	J	D	C	U	R	R	E	N	T	Y	I	E	L	D	R
U	P	A	X	N	L	A	D	V	E	R	T	I	S	E	M	E	N	T	Y
N	R	L	D	D	E	C	L	A	R	A	T	I	O	N	D	A	T	E	Y
F	I	E	K	G	N	H	K	B	U	S	I	N	E	S	S	D	A	Y	A
V	C	R	L	S	C	O	M	M	O	N	S	T	O	C	K	H	E	T	P
R	E	O	J	B	E	S	T	E	F	F	O	R	T	S	Q	U	U	G	E

1. Family of funds, mutual fund complex
2. The sale of investment company shares in amounts just below the point at which the sales charge is reduced on quantity.
3. The date on which the company declares an upcoming dividend.
4. Allows the firm working for the issuing company to sell its shares the best way they can and are not responsible if shares are not sold.
5. A type of best efforts underwriting where the entire amount must be sold or the deal is called off.
6. A day the New York Stock Exchange is open for business (trading).
7. Selection risk, business risk
8. One who deals in securities as a principal, buying and selling for his own account.
9. The basic stock issued by a corporation representing shares of ownership.
10. Alternative Minimum Tax. The requirement to add the income from tax preference items to income above an indexed level. A method to insure that wealthy persons and corporations pay at least some tax.
11. The price at which the dealer is willing to sell the stock to an investor or another dealer.
12. The yield of the security when bought or sold prior to maturity in the secondary market. Current yield relates current income to the security's current price.
13. Any promotional material designed for use by newspapers, magazines, billboards, radio, television, telephone recordings or other public media.
14. State securities laws.
15. Ad Valorem tax
16. A market in which prices of securities are moving higher or are expected to move higher.
17. Broker-dealer firm primarily on the NASDAQ that opens bids and sells a particular security, taking on the risk of selling that security.
18. Cash equivalents such as T-bills, CDs, commercial paper, BAs; Preservation of Capital; attempts to maintain $1 NAV ; used to park funds while making investment decisions.

A. Business Day
E. Ask Price
I. Current Yield
M. Market Maker
Q. Money Market Fund

B. Blue Sky Laws
F. Non-systematic risk
J. AMT
N. Declaration Date
R. Best Efforts

C. Mutual Fund Family
G. Advertisement
K. All or None
O. Dealer

D. Breakpoint Sale
H. Property tax
L. Common Stock
P. Bull Market

12. *Find the hidden words. The words have been placed horizontally, vertically, or diagonally. When you locate a word, draw a circle around it.*

L	I	Q	U	I	D	I	T	Y	O	B	J	E	C	T	I	V	E	N	L
N	E	B	B	A	N	K	E	R	S	A	C	C	E	P	T	A	N	C	E
A	C	O	L	L	A	T	E	R	A	L	T	R	U	S	T	B	O	N	D
K	B	L	U	E	C	H	I	P	S	T	O	C	K	Z	O	T	C	V	Y
E	F	O	A	G	P	K	P	Q	A	N	N	U	I	T	A	N	T	L	S
D	F	I	F	I	N	S	I	D	E	R	C	O	V	E	R	D	E	L	L
H	Y	C	Z	X	F	P	R	E	P	A	Y	M	E	N	T	R	I	S	K
F	Y	C	A	I	C	A	P	I	T	A	L	G	A	I	N	S	J	S	B
X	U	I	S	F	L	O	N	G	K	E	P	R	E	M	I	U	M	X	F
E	G	X	K	D	C	U	R	R	E	N	T	Y	I	E	L	D	F	C	Y
X	A	F	F	I	L	I	A	T	E	D	P	E	R	S	O	N	X	P	L
A	W	O	J	E	E	U	P	Z	D	B	S	H	A	R	E	S	F	I	X

1. Uncovered
2. Fixed-Income Securities: Possibility that homeowners will prepay mortgages more quickly than expected when interest rates fall.
3. Bank End Load
4. This is a primary need for those who never know when they will need cash quickly.
5. Form of debt backed by stocks and or bonds of another corporation. The collateral is held by a trustee for safekeeping.
6. The stock of normally strong, well-established companies that have demonstrated their ability to pay dividends in good times and bad times.
7. Anyone in a position to influence decisions made in a corporation, including officers, directors, principal stockholders, and members of their immediate families.
8. Over the counter. A negotiated market.
9. To offer
10. Bonds that cost more than the face value.
11. The yield of the security when bought or sold prior to maturity in the secondary market. Current yield relates current income to the security's current price.
12. Control person, affiliate
13. Person who receives an annuity contract's distribution.
14. Educational IRA
15. The long-term gain on an asset hold for a period of longer than 12 months.
16. Buy, bought, hold, or own
17. Essentially a letter of credit from a bank guaranteeing payment of a debt.
18. Mix of equities and bonds.

A. Liquidity Objective
E. Premium
I. Capital Gain
M. Blue Chip Stock
Q. Long

B. Collateral Trust Bond
F. Affiliated Person
J. B shares
N. Growth & Income Fund
R. Coverdell

C. Naked
G. Current Yield
K. Prepayment Risk
O. Insider

D. Annuitant
H. Bankers Acceptance
L. OTC
P. Ask

13. *Find the hidden words. The words have been placed horizontally, vertically, or diagonally. When you locate a word, draw a circle around it.*

X	I	R	V	B	R	E	A	K	P	O	I	N	T	S	A	L	E	P	C
C	U	M	U	L	A	T	I	V	E	V	O	T	I	N	G	A	C	A	M
U	D	A	M	O	R	T	I	Z	A	T	I	O	N	I	B	R	S	R	U
A	C	C	R	U	E	D	I	N	T	E	R	E	S	T	V	B	H	V	C
C	R	E	D	I	T	R	I	S	K	U	Z	C	Z	E	K	I	A	A	C
O	T	C	X	D	E	B	E	N	T	U	R	E	R	F	J	T	R	L	L
B	R	O	K	E	R	S	E	C	T	O	R	F	U	N	D	R	E	U	E
B	P	P	B	L	U	E	C	H	I	P	S	T	O	C	K	A	S	E	X
C	A	M	T	A	C	C	O	U	N	T	E	X	E	C	U	T	I	V	E
Y	L	I	Q	U	I	D	I	T	Y	O	B	J	E	C	T	I	V	E	Y
Z	F	W	L	A	P	P	R	E	C	I	A	T	I	O	N	O	D	U	L
U	H	B	A	N	K	E	R	S	A	C	C	E	P	T	A	N	C	E	S

1. The stated value of a security, referring to preferred stocks and bonds that the issuer is willing to pay the investor when the bond matures.
2. The interest that has accumulated since the last interest payment up to, but not including, the settlement date, and that is added to a bond transaction's contract price.
3. The sale of investment company shares in amounts just below the point at which the sales charge is reduced on quantity.
4. A process that allows industry disputes between members, member organizations, their employees, and customers to be heard and settled by either FINRA or a designated arbitration panel.
5. Registered Representative
6. Alternative Minimum Tax. The requirement to add the income from tax preference items to income above an indexed level. A method to insure that wealthy persons and corporations pay at least some tax.
7. A type of shareholder voting in which the number of shares held is multiplied by the number of directors to be elected to determine the number of votes a shareholder may cast.
8. Over the counter. A negotiated market.
9. This is a primary need for those who never know when they will need cash quickly.
10. Payment of a debt (principal) over a period of time in periodic installments.
11. Essentially a letter of credit from a bank guaranteeing payment of a debt.
12. The increase in value of an asset. Sometimes called growth.
13. Common stock from particular industry.
14. Level Load
15. unsecured Bond backed only by the good faith of the corporation. Repayment of the debt is based on the company's promise to repay.
16. Possibility that principal or interest will not be paid.
17. The stock of normally strong, well-established companies that have demonstrated their ability to pay dividends in good times and bad times.
18. The role of a brokerage firm when it acts as an agent for a customer and charges the customer a commission for its services.

A. C shares
B. Par Value
C. Broker
D. OTC
E. Sector Fund
F. Breakpoint Sale
G. Blue Chip Stock
H. Bankers Acceptance
I. Account Executive
J. Appreciation
K. Cumulative Voting
L. Accrued Interest
M. Credit Risk
N. Debenture
O. Arbitration
P. Liquidity Objective
Q. AMT
R. Amortization

14. *Find the hidden words. The words have been placed horizontally, vertically, or diagonally. When you locate a word, draw a circle around it.*

U	A	N	N	U	I	T	Y	B	R	O	K	E	R	U	N	B	K	V	M
C	A	L	L	P	R	I	C	E	B	E	A	R	M	A	R	K	E	T	Z
T	I	M	I	N	G	R	I	S	K	Y	V	F	A	G	D	I	K	Y	K
F	C	O	N	D	U	I	T	T	H	E	O	R	Y	O	L	Z	V	X	D
O	D	A	U	C	T	I	O	N	M	A	R	K	E	T	S	R	W	K	Z
I	Q	Y	B	A	L	A	N	C	E	D	F	U	N	D	L	O	X	D	R
U	C	A	C	C	U	M	U	L	A	T	I	O	N	S	T	A	G	E	X
D	D	S	A	M	O	R	T	I	Z	A	T	I	O	N	Z	Z	S	C	S
W	A	P	S	H	U	P	A	Y	M	E	N	T	D	A	T	E	Z	Q	Y
S	P	E	C	I	A	L	S	I	T	U	A	T	I	O	N	F	U	N	D
W	L	I	Q	U	I	D	I	T	Y	R	I	S	K	R	V	D	O	W	X
K	H	S	U	I	N	D	E	X	F	U	N	D	M	V	T	K	M	N	V

1. A market where sellers bid for stock and buyers sell their stock.
2. Equity Category; Portfolio: common stock in same proportions as selected index.
3. Payment of a debt (principal) over a period of time in periodic installments.
4. Investing in a specific security at an inopportune time. Dollar cost averaging is used to avoid this risk.
5. Possible large gain if situation plays out as manager predicts; Depends on ability of manager to find special deals.
6. A theory behind Subchapter M under which distributions to shareholders are not taxed to the investment company.
7. The date the company mails out the dividend.
8. The role of a brokerage firm when it acts as an agent for a customer and charges the customer a commission for its services.
9. Mix of equities and bonds; growth with opportunity for income; portfolio mix usually under tighter constraints than growth & income fund.
10. Ability to quickly sell an investment at or near current market price. Regardless of type, more heavily traded securities are more liquid.
11. The period during which contributions are made to an annuity account.
12. A market in which prices of securities are falling or are expected to fall.
13. Front end sales charge, front end load
14. The price paid for callable preferred stock or bonds redeemed by the issuer prior to maturity of the issue because interest rates have fallen.
15. An accounting measure used to determine the amount of each payment during an annuity's distribution stage.
16. A contract between an insurance company and an individual, generally guaranteeing lifetime income to the individual.
17. Wholesaler, sponsor, underwriter

A. Annuity Unit
E. Balanced Fund
I. Distributor
M. Special Situation Fund
Q. Liquidity Risk
B. Broker
F. Payment date
J. Bear Market
N. Amortization
C. Class A shares
G. Call Price
K. Conduit Theory
O. Accumulation Stage
D. Index Fund
H. Auction markets
L. Annuity
P. Timing Risk

15. *Find the hidden words. The words have been placed horizontally, vertically, or diagonally. When you locate a word, draw a circle around it.*

S	E	D	O	C	O	N	T	R	A	C	T	U	A	L	P	L	A	N	K
P	D	C	N	Y	S	X	B	R	Q	A	L	L	O	R	N	O	N	E	P
G	E	O	V	C	B	R	E	A	K	P	O	I	N	T	S	A	L	E	H
D	A	R	N	E	T	A	S	S	E	T	V	A	L	U	E	U	P	G	V
E	L	P	P	D	R	A	T	B	A	L	A	N	C	E	D	F	U	N	D
A	L	O	I	U	F	B	E	G	F	F	U	Y	H	M	U	H	G	F	Z
L	O	R	A	R	X	F	F	M	U	T	U	A	L	F	U	N	D	Q	
E	R	A	B	A	E	G	F	Q	Y	G	L	O	B	A	L	F	U	N	D
R	N	T	H	T	F	S	O	A	G	L	J	O	X	A	S	S	E	T	K
G	O	I	X	I	M	R	R	M	N	R	X	R	H	U	J	O	W	B	V
O	N	O	J	O	P	C	T	T	B	Y	A	N	N	U	I	T	Y	D	Z
K	E	N	I	N	X	A	S	A	N	N	U	A	L	R	E	T	U	R	N

1. Mix of equities and bonds; growth with opportunity for income; portfolio mix usually under tighter constraints than growth & income fund.
2. Allows the firm working for the issuing company to sell its shares the best way they can and are not responsible if shares are not sold.
3. The sale of investment company shares in amounts just below the point at which the sales charge is reduced on quantity.
4. The price of a mutual fund. Calculates to company's funds minus liabilities divided by outstanding shares.
5. A form of business organization in which the total worth of the organization is divided into shares of stock.
6. Alternative Minimum Tax. The requirement to add the income from tax preference items to income above an indexed level. A method to insure that wealthy persons and corporations pay at least some tax.
7. States that the issuing company wants ALL (or nothing) the shares to be sold if not, the underwriting is cancelled.
8. Possible large gain if situation plays out as manager predicts; Depends on ability of manager to find special deals.
9. Common stock from inside and outside the U.S. Capital appreciation in whatever markets look attractive to manager.
10. Open end management company.
11. Measure of the bond price in relations to the time the bond end. Taking in consideration the interest-rates, time to maturity, and differences between the coupon rate and the yield to maturity.
12. Principal
13. Holding period return
14. Also called period payment plans.
15. A type of best efforts underwriting where the entire amount must be sold or the deal is called off.
16. Anything that an individual or a corporation owns.
17. A contract between an insurance company and an individual. An annuity generally guarantees lifetime income to the person on whose life the contract is based.

A. Balanced Fund	B. Duration	C. Net Asset Value	D. Mutual Fund
E. Special Situation Fund	F. Asset	G. Corporation	H. Global Fund
I. Best Efforts	J. All or none	K. Annuity	L. All or None
M. Breakpoint Sale	N. Dealer	O. Contractual Plan	P. Annual return
Q. AMT			

Glossary

Advertisement: Any material designed for use by newspapers, magazines, radio, television, telephone, recordings or any other public medium to solicit business.

Affiliated Person: Includes an investment adviser, officer, director, partner or employee of another person.

Agency Debt: Often called "Indirect Debt."

Aggressive Growth Portfolio: Portfolio characterized by high turnover of holdings, attempts to cash in on higher-risk rapid capital appreciation situations.

Aggressive Investment Policy: A policy concentrating on maximum return. Such a policy entails increased risks.

Amortization: Payment of a debt (principal) over a period of time in periodic installments.

Annuitant: The annuity contract holder.

Annuity: A contract between an insurance company and an individual. An annuity generally guarantees lifetime income to the person on whose life the contract is based.

Annuity Unit: The accounting measure used to determine the amount of each payment to an annuitant during the pay-out period.

Appreciation: The increase in value of an asset. Sometimes called growth.

Ask Price: The price at which the dealer is willing to sell the stock to an investor or another dealer.

Assumed Interest Rate: A base for illustrating payments from a variable annuity.

Auction Market: A stock exchange where the securities are sold to the highest bidder.

Authorized Stock: Authorized stock is the maximum number of shares a corporation may issue under the terms of its charter.

Balanced Fund: A type of mutual fund that at all times some portion of its investment assets in bonds and stocks, creating a balance between the two types of securities.

Bankers Acceptance: Essentially a letter of credit from a bank guaranteeing payment of a debt.

Bear Market: A market in which prices of securities are falling or are expected to fall.

Best Efforts Underwriting: Acting as an agent for the issuer, the underwriter puts forth his or her best efforts to sell as many shares as possible.

Bid Price: The price at which a dealer is willing to buy stock from an individual or another dealer.

Blue Chip Stock: The stock of normally strong, well-established companies that have demonstrated their ability to pay dividends in good times and bad times.

Blue Sky Laws: State securities laws.

Bond: Represent the borrowing of money by a corporation or government.

Bond Fund: A type of mutual fund whose investment policy is to provide stable income with a minimum of capital risks.

Bond Rating: The quality of a bond issue as determined by independent bond rating services. AAA being of the highest quality.

Breakpoint: The schedule of sales charge discounts offered by a mutual fund for lump sum or cumulative investments. Eligibility requirements must be disclosed in the prospectus.

Breakpoint Sale: The sale of investment company shares in amounts just below the point at which the sales charge is reduced on quantity.

Broker: The role of a brokerage firm when it acts as an agent for a customer and charges the customer a commission for its services.

Bull Market: A market in which prices of securities are moving higher or are expected to move higher.

Business Day: A day the New York Stock Exchange is open for business (trading).

Call Option: An option to buy a specified number of shares of stock at a definite price within a specified period of time. See put option.

Call Price: The price paid for callable preferred stock or bonds redeemed by the issuer prior to maturity of the issue because interest rates have fallen.

Call Provisions: An issuing corporation retains the privilege of recalling (redeeming) its issues of equity or debt.

Capital Gain: The long-term gain on an asset hold for a period of longer than 12 months.

Capital Structure: The amount of debt or equity issued by a corporation.

Certification of Deposit: Issued by most commercial banks, representing bank borrowing for a short period of time.

Churning: Excessive trading in a customer's account. The registered representative ignores the objectives and interest of clients and seeks only to increase commissions.

Code of Arbitrations: Provides a method of handling securities-related disputes or clearing controversies between members, public customers, clearing corporations or clearing banks.

Code of Procedure: FINRA's procedures for handling trade practice complaints.

Collateral Trust Bond: Form of debt backed by stocks and or bonds of another corporation. The collateral is held by a trustee for safekeeping.

Combined Annuity: An annuity combining the features of the fixed and variable annuities.

Commercial Paper: A corporate money market instrument which consists of signed promissory notes issued by the corporation to raise short-term funds.

Common Stock: The basic stock issued by a corporation representing shares of ownership.

Conduit Theory: A theory behind Subchapter M under which distributions to shareholders are not taxed to the investment company.

Constant dollars: Dollars adjusted to show the same purchasing power from one period to another. They are "indexed" for inflation.

Contractual Plan: Also called period payment plans.

Contractual Plan Company: A unit investment trust with which an investor may contact to buy mutual fund shares at fixed intervals over a fixed period of time.

Convertible Bond: A bond that may be exchanged for some other security of the issuer at the option of the holder. It is usually converted into common stock based upon a fixed conversion ratio.

Convertible Preferred Stock: Preferred stock that may be converted into common stock at the option of the holder.

Cooling off Period: Traditionally, the 20-day period between the filing date of a registration statement and the effective date of the registration.

Corporation: A form of business organization in which the total worth of the organization is divided into shares of stock.

Cost Basis: Money on which taxes have been paid. A return of cost basis is a return of capital and not subject to tax.

Coupon Rate: Nominal Yield

Cumulative Preferred: Has the right to receive skipped or missed dividends.

Cumulative Voting: A type of shareholder voting in which the number of shares held is multiplied by the number of directors to be elected to determine the number of votes a shareholder may cast.

Current Dollars: Actual dollar amounts. Not adjusted for inflation.

Current Yield: The yield of the security when bought or sold prior to maturity in the secondary market. Current yield relates current income to the security's current price.

Custodian: The Investment Company Act of 1940 requires the fund's assets be held by an independent custodian.

Dealer: One who deals in securities as a principal, buying and selling for his own account.

Debenture: unsecured Bond backed only by the good faith of the corporation. Repayment of the debt is based on the company's promise to repay.

Declaration Date: The date on which the company declares an upcoming dividend.

Money Market Fund: Cash equivalents such as T-bills, CDs, commercial paper, BAs; Preservation of Capital; attempts to maintain $1 NAV ; used to park funds while making investment decisions.

US Goverment Fund: T-bonds, T-notes, T-bills; Income with no credit risk; may be subject to interest rate risk; the longer average maturity of the portfolio the greater the interest rate risk

Municipal Bond Fund: Income that is free from federal, and possibly state income tax; higher the investor's tax bracket, the more beneficial the tax exemption; may have some default risk; interest rate risk.

Corporate Investment Grade Fund: Corporate bonds rated BBB:Baa or higher; Income with modest credit risk; Dividends are fully taxable; Interest rate risk

Corporate High Yield Fund: Corporate bonds rate BB:Ba or lower; Higher than normal income with higher than normal default risk; Investor must be able and willing to assume default risk; Also has interest rate risk

Growth & Income Fund: Mix of equities and bonds.

Balanced Fund: Mix of equities and bonds; growth with opportunity for income; portfolio mix usually under tighter constraints than growth & income fund.

Equity Income Fund: Dividend paying equities; safe, consistent income with secondary objective of growth; less volatile than other equity funds.

Growth Fund: Common stock; capital appreciation; income not a consideration; subject to market fluctuations.

Aggressive Growth Fund: Small cap stocks; maximum capital appreciation; may employ short-term trading strategies; very volatile.

Index Fund: Equity Category; Portfolio: common stock in same proportions as selected index.

International Fund: Common stocks from outside of the U.S.; Exposure to exchange rate risk and political (legistlative) risk, in addition to market risk.

Global Fund: Common stock from inside and outside the U.S. Capital appreciation in whatever markets look attractive to manager.

Sector Fund: Common stock from particular industry.

Special Situation Fund: Possible large gain if situation plays out as manager predicts; Depends on ability of manager to find special deals.

Growth Objective: Investment objective for increase in invested capital, primarily generated through price appreciation. Equity securities (stocks) are usually used in pursuit of this goal.

Income Objective: Investment objective for regular production of cash from investments, through dividend or interest payments. Bonds and preferred stocks are often used to produce income.

Total Return Objective: Investment objective for a combination of growth of capital and income, but less of each than investments that focus on just one of those objectives.

Tax Reduction Objective: Investment objective for high-bracket investors facing a big tax bite on taxable investments may find tax-exempt vehicles produce a better after tax return.

Speculation Objective: Investment objective for investors that are willing and able to take considerable risks for the chance to hit a big financial home run.

Liquidity Objective: This is a primary need for those who never know when they will need cash quickly.

Capital Risk: General term for possible loss of money invested. This risk is present in most securities.

Timing Risk: Investing in a specific security at an inopportune time. Dollar cost averaging is used to avoid this risk.

Market Risk: Possible loss of value due to a broad market decline. For equities, this risk is measured by a statistic called beta.

Liquidity Risk: Ability to quickly sell an investment at or near current market price. Regardless of type, more heavily traded securities are more liquid.

Political Risk: Changes in laws or rules may have negative impact on investments. The common wisdom is that political risk is high anytime Congress is in session.

Currency Risk: Changes in value of a currency versus another currency. Current owners of forign securities may see a negative impact if foreign currency weakens against their home currency.

Opportunity Cost Risk: Loss of income or appreciation because an investment was NOT made.

Credit Risk: Possibility that principal or interest will not be paid.

Interest Rate Risk: Possibility that increase in general level of interest rates will drive down prices of existing fixed-income investments.

Inflationary Risk:Rise in general level of prices reduces the value of fixed returns.

Call Risk: Bonds are more likely to be called when rates have dropped, forcing reinvestment of principal at lower rates.

Prepayment Risk: Fixed-Income Securities: Possibility that homeowners will prepay mortgages more quickly than expected when interest rates fall.

American Depository Receipt: American Depository Shares

Annual return: Holding period return

Ask: To offer

Authorized stock: "New" stock

B shares: Bank End Load

Back end sales charge: Contingent deferred sales charge (CDSC)

Bondholder: A creditor

Broker: An agent

Brokerage fee: Sales Charge, Sales Load

Buy: Own, Hold, Purchase, Long

C shares: Level Load

Capital Risk: Principal Risk

Class A shares: Front end sales charge, front end load

Contribution: Cost basis

Corporate Charter: Articles of Incorporation

Coverdell: Educational IRA

Credit risk: Default risk

Dealer: Principal

Distributor: Wholesaler, sponsor, underwriter

Equity income fund: Growth and income fund

Exchange: Switch

Exchange market: Auction market

Income bond: Adjustment bond

Insider: Control person, affiliate

Investment income: interest & dividends

Keogh Plan: An HR-10 retirement Plan

Long: Buy, bought, hold, or own

Market risk: Systematic risk

Municipal bonds: Tax-free bonds

Mutual Fund: Open end management company.

Mutual Fund Family: Family of funds, mutual fund complex

Naked: Uncovered

Net yield: After-tax yield

Nominal yield: Coupon, coupon rate, interest

Non-systematic risk: Selection risk, business risk

Outstanding shares: Shares held by the public

OTC: Over the counter. A negotiated market.

Par value: Face amount, principal

Preliminary prospectus: Red Herring

Pre-tax: Tax- deductible

Primary market: New issue market, primary distribution, sold by prospectus only.

Progressive tax: Graduated tax, income tax

Property tax: Ad Valorem tax

Auction markets: A market where sellers bid for stock and buyers sell their stock.

Specialist: Auctioneer of the stock, sets the opening bid, facilitates the trade between brokers and dealers, and makes sure the best bid for the stock is executed and sold.

Floor Broker: Buys stocks for its clients and for personal needs based on their listing price on the floor.

Primary Market: Where new issues of stock are issued. The only time when issuing companies make a profit on their shares.

Market Maker: Broker-dealer firm primarily on the NASDAQ that opens bids and sells a particular security, taking on the risk of selling that security.

Spread: Is the price difference the Market Maker is willing to buy the stock for, to the amount he:she gets for the stock when sold.

IPO: Primary Offering. New issues that are offered in the primary market and are sold to the public for the first time.

Investment Banker: Introduces new securities to the market, that advises the issuing company of the price the security will be sold for to the public.

Firm Commitment: Bank buys issuing companies shares and sells them on the market for commission. Shares are not owned by the banks.

Best Efforts: Allows the firm working for the issuing company to sell its shares the best way they can and are not responsible if shares are not sold.

All or none: States that the issuing company wants ALL (or nothing) the shares to be sold if not, the underwriting is cancelled.

Standby: Allows the Underwriting firm to purchase any shares that the issuing company's shareholders have not bought and sell the shares themselves for a profit.

Trade date: Date transaction is executed.

Settlement date: Date transaction is completed and the seller pays buyer and the buyer receives the shares.

Regular way Settlement Date: Refers to Corporate stocks:bonds, Municipal bonds is three days after the trade date.

Declaration Date: The date the Board of Directors announces intention of paying dividends.

Record Date:Date where the BOD checks if a shareholder is listed with the company, so they can get paid their dividends.

Ex dividend Date: The date the security trades without its dividends. In order to get a dividend the security needs to be purchased two days prior to the record date or before the ex-dividend date.

Payment date: The date the company mails out the dividend.

Market Value: Current bid and asking price of security.

Bid: The price a Market Maker will pay for a security; it's the price an investor would receive if he or she sold the security.

Asked: This is the price an investor would pay when buying the security.

Net Asset Value: The price of a mutual fund. Calculates to company's funds minus liabilities divided by outstanding shares.

Par Value: The stated value of a security, referring to preferred stocks and bonds that the issuer is willing to pay the investor when the bond matures.

Discount: Bonds that are sold less then par value.

Premium: Bonds that cost more than the face value.

Nominal yield: Yield stated on the bonds coupon.

Yield to maturity: Calculation of a bonds total return if held until the end of its life (maturity).

Duration: Measure of the bond price in relations to the time the bond end. Taking in consideration the interest-rates, time to maturity, and differences between the coupon rate and the yield to maturity.

Current yield: Present yield the buyer would receive when purchasing the bond. Calculated by dividing Annual Interest rates to Market Price.

Account Executive: Registered Representative

Accredited Investor: Any institution or an individual meeting minimum net worth requirements for the purchase of securities qualifying under the Regulation D registration exemption.

Accrued Interest: The interest that has accumulated since the last interest payment up to, but not including, the settlement date, and that is added to a bond transaction's contract price.

Accumulation Stage: The period during which contributions are made to an annuity account.

Accumulation Unit: An accounting measure used to determine an annuitant's proportionate interest in the insurer's separate account during an annuity's accumulation (deposit) stage.

AGI: Adjusted Gross Income. Earned income plus net passive income, portfolio income, and capital gains.

Administrator: A person authorized by a court of law to liquidate an intestate decedent's estate.

Advertisement: Any promotional material designed for use by newspapers, magazines, billboards, radio, television, telephone recordings or other public media.

Affiliated Person: Anyone in a position to influence decisions made in a corporation, including officers, directors, principal stockholders, and members of their immediate families.

Agency Basis: An agency Transaction

Agency Issue: A debt security issued by an authorized agency of the federal government.

Agency Transaction: A transaction in which a broker or dealer acts for the accounts of others by buying or selling securities on behalf of customers.

Agent: An individual or a firm that effects securities transactions for the accounts of others.

Aggressive Investment Agency: A method of portfolio allocation and management aimed at achieving maximum return.

All or None: A type of best efforts underwriting where the entire amount must be sold or the deal is called off.

AMT: Alternative Minimum Tax. The requirement to add the income from tax preference items to income above an indexed level. A method to insure that wealthy persons and corporations pay at least some tax.

American Depositary Receipt: A negotiable certificate representing a given number of shares of stock in a foreign corporation.

Annual Compliance Review: The annual meeting that all registered representatives and principals must attend, the purpose of which is to review compliance issues.

Annual Report: A formal statement issued yearly by a corporation to its share-owners. It shows assets, liabilities, equity revenues, expenses, and so forth.

Annuitant: Person who receives an annuity contract's distribution.

Annuitize: To change an annuity contract from the accumulation (pay-in) stage to the distribution (payout) stage.

Annuity: A contract between an insurance company and an individual, generally guaranteeing lifetime income to the individual.

Annuity Unit: An accounting measure used to determine the amount of each payment during an annuity's distribution stage.

Appreciation: The increase in an asset's value.

Arbitrage: The technique of buying and selling the same financial instrument in two different markets simultaneously to take advantage of a momentary price disparity.

Arbitration: A process that allows industry disputes between members, member organizations, their employees, and customers to be heard and settled by either FINRA or a designated arbitration panel.

Ask: An indication of willingness by a trader or dealer to sell a security or a commodity.

Asset: Anything that an individual or a corporation owns.

Asset Allocation Fund: A mutual fund that splits its investment assets among stocks, bonds, and other vehicles in an attempt to provide a consistent return for the investor.

Asset Backed Security: A debt security backed by a loan, lease or receivables against assets other than real estate and mortgage-backed securities.

Assignment: A document accompanying or part of a stock certificate that is signed by the person named on the certificate for the purpose of transferring the certificate's title to another person's name.

Assumed Interest Rate: The net rate of investment return that must be credited to a variable life insurance policy to ensure that at all times the variable death benefit equals the amount of the death benefit.

Auction Market: A market in which buyers enter competitive bids and sellers enter competitive offers simultaneously.

Authorized Stock: The number of shares of stock that a corporation may issue.

Automatic Reinvestment: An option available to mutual fund shareholders whereby fund dividends and capital gains distributions are automatically reinvested back into the fund.

Average: A price at a midpoint among a number of prices. Technical analysts often use averages as market indicators.

Average Price: A bond's average price is calculated by adding its face value to the price paid for it and dividing the result by two.

Made in the USA
Columbia, SC
22 October 2020